Youth Group Trust Builders

BY DENNY RYDBERG

Loveland, Colorado

DEDICATION

To my youngest son, Jonathan, who
at 8 years of age, is a real community builder.

ACKNOWLEDGMENTS

I want to thank those who inspired and labored on *Building Community in Youth Groups,* especially Ken Beebe, Robin Dursch, Paul Evans, and the rest of the gang from Reachout Expeditions, an organization that does a tremendous job using the wilderness to reach out to youth. Reachout's address is Box 464, Anacortes, Washington 98221.

I want to thank my fellow staffer and good friend, Craig Goodwin, who did a great deal of the research with me on this one.

I want to thank my family and my colleagues at University Presbyterian Church. Any time you write a book, your family and colleagues also write a book!

Finally, I want to thank the competent and enthusiastic team at Group for doing such a great job.

Youth Group Trust Builders

Copyright © 1993 Denny Rydberg

Scripture quoted from The Youth Bible, New Century Version, copyright © 1991 by Word Publishing, Dallas, Texas 75039. Used by permission.

Credits
Edited by Stephen Parolini
Designed by Lisa Smith
Cover design by Liz Howe
Cover illustration by Joel Armstrong
Cover photography by David Priest

Library of Congress Cataloging-in-Publication Data
Rydberg, Denny.
    Youth group trust builders / by Denny Rydberg.
       p.   cm.
    ISBN 1-55945-172-6
    1. Church work with teenagers. I. Title.
BV4447.R933   1993
259'.23—dc20   92-40663
                                            CIP

13 12 11 10 9 8 7 6   04 03 02 01 00 99 98 97
Printed in the United States of America.

CONTENTS

CHAPTER THREE:

OPENING UP

CHAPTER FOUR:

AFFIRMING

CHAPTER FIVE:

CHAPTER SIX:

INTRODUCTION

I n 1985 I wrote a book with Ken Beebe, Robin Dursch, and others called *Building Community in Youth Groups*.

The book grew out of the discovery that when you take a group of teenagers on a wilderness trip and "force" them into situations in which they're required to work as a team, the teenagers develop a strong sense of community. A collection of wilderness hikers becomes a committed team, a family, a real group.

In that first book we took what we'd learned in the wilderness and transferred those concepts to the classroom. We designed activities that forced people to be involved but didn't force them to move too quickly beyond their abilities. We designed a series of five steps that would help people progressively share and care for one another.

Youth workers told me in person and through letters that the principles and activities were helpful and worked. The first book, which is still in print and which I still recommend heartily, has been used by over 40,000 youth workers and by probably over a million students.

In my travels around the country speaking and meeting with youth workers, I was told it was time to come up with more strategies for building community and trust in youth groups. This book is my answer to those requests.

A key player in the development of *this* book has been Craig Goodwin. Craig served with me as an intern in our ministry to college students. Craig also has experience as a youth director with high school and junior high students and as a recreation director with elementary school children in a city-sponsored program. As of the printing of this book, Craig is in seminary in California.

I hope that you'll be able to take the content of this book and, with your own creativity and prayers, create a climate in which community takes place—a climate in which young people mature in their desire to love, serve, and obey the Lord.

Denny Rydberg

Some youth groups are more accurately described as "mobs," "crowds," or simply "collections of individuals." They really don't have any group identity at all.

A youth group is a complex organism—and often more a collection of self-conscious individuals than a committed group of caring, sharing, loving people. This truism applies to youth groups of any size— small as well as large. It applies to groups within highly structured programs and to freewheeling, "wing-it" youth ministries. It applies to groups in Bellingham and in Bermuda.

But youth groups don't have to be collections of self-serving teenagers. With the proper program design, youth groups can become close-knit communities regardless of their size, situation, or location. A group of five can effectively learn and grow together. And a group of 500 can become a caring, sharing, loving community, too.

The key to building community is to create an environment where community can take place. But before we explore ways to create community, we must explore the dynamics at work in our youth groups.

UNDERSTANDING THE DYNAMICS OF A YOUTH GROUP

The first dynamic, leadership, can work for or against you in building community. Every youth group has at least a few leaders whether they're officially elected or self-appointed. Mature leaders will aid in community building. But immature leaders can destroy the sense of cohesiveness and community that may already exist. We need strategies that work with all kinds of leadership—strategies that *involve* leaders, followers, and rebels in the process of building community. The activities in this book apply to all kinds of leaders—and the groups they lead.

The second dynamic, motivation, often directly affects the success of our community-building attempts. What motivates teenagers to attend youth group meetings and events? Some kids are coerced into attending by well-meaning parents and would rather be at home. Some are motivated by boredom, the desire for fun times, or the search for relationships with members of the opposite sex. Some are just looking for friends. And, yes, some attend because they believe in what's going on and want to learn and grow. The strategies in this book are designed to help teenagers with each of these motivations discover and experience a sense of community.

Confidence is the third dynamic. Some teenagers would love to share what's going on in their lives with a caring group of friends, but they don't have the confidence or the competence to share such things. They need help. And others who are articulate when it comes to concepts, choke up when it comes to personal sharing. They, too, need a way to gradually become more open and confident with a group that cares.

The fourth dynamic is emotional and spiritual health. Some of your kids have intense hurts and deep scars. They want help, but they've been beaten up in the past, and their vulnerability level is low. Some teenagers are spiritually mature while others are spiritual infants. This wide diversity makes learning and sharing difficult. We need strategies to give people from different emotional and spiritual backgrounds a common experience so that sharing can take place. The activities in this book provide you with effective ways to include all kinds of kids in community building.

The fifth dynamic is energy. Most teenagers prefer activity to lecture. And that makes sense—kids learn best by doing, by being involved in *discovering* nuggets of truth rather than being told *about* the truth. In this book, community building begins with action. In each activity we take advantage of kids' love for activity to help them get into a theme that will help them grow closer to each other and God.

MAKING SENSE OF THE WHIRLWIND

Beyond their obvious diversity, teenagers have much in common. They're working (sometimes stumbling) through adolescence. They're concerned with their bodies. They're testing the limits of their intellects. They're adventurers. They're risk takers. They're searching for a real faith that works. They have big questions. They have thoughtful answers. They're gifted and have great potential. They face tremendous peer pressure.

They're loved by God.

And you're in the middle of this whirlwind. Out of these complicated dynamics—this swirling mix of independence, pain, despair, and hope—you must create a climate that is safe and adventuresome at the same time, a place where people can be stretched but in such a manner that they aren't scared away or deeply hurt in the process.

This might seem like an impossible task. Yet, despite the incredible diversity within youth groups, common ground does exist to help these collections of individuals become healthy, caring groups. All the right stuff is there. And the Lord is on our side, a comforting thought when the ministry seems hard.

However, teenagers won't become a community automatically or overnight. It takes time to develop community. And it takes the work of the Holy Spirit—meeting each individual and helping to mold all of the individuals into a community. We, the youth leaders, can help to create a climate where community can grow.

I've identified five steps that can help create that climate. Each step can help kids put down their armor and begin to build trust within the group.

1 BOND BUILDING

The first step in building community is to break down cliques and barriers and to establish trust among the students. One way this can be accomplished is by giving group members problem-solving tasks which require them to work side by side with others in the group.

As they discuss solutions and physically help one another to accomplish the task, group members build bonds regardless of their differences before the activity. Cooperation is the main goal in step one, for cooperation leads to the beginning of a *team* feeling. The activities in the chapter on bond building are, for the most part, short, active, and fun. They focus on group interaction and make group building easily observable. Turn to page 17 for the bond-building activities.

2 OPENING UP

When an individual begins to share nonthreatening areas of his or her life, an exciting step in group building takes place. Most people like to talk about themselves if the situation is safe—if they know that what they say is accepted and that they are, too. If teenagers perceive that other group members are generally interested in them, they can trust the group enough to share. But if they perceive that others don't care to listen, no trust is built.

With that in mind, the exercises in step two are designed to get people to *begin* sharing and listening to each other. The exercises are generic enough to let students share to the degree they feel comfortable. The goal is to have students walk away feeling enthusiastic about the deepening friendships they're developing. In these exercises, kids discover that personal imperfections are not unique, that "we're all in this together," and that other people care for them. The opening-up exercises begin on page 55.

3 AFFIRMING

Crucial to the growth process of the group is the act of encouraging or affirming. When a guy hears honest compliments from his peers, he enjoys participating in the group much more and is likely to share more in the future. When a young woman is told by her friends that they appreciate her, her self-worth increases dramatically.

Many reclusive students become active participants in the group when they realize that others truly care. But most of us are not good at affirmations. So we need practice in giving and receiving affirmations. We also need to create a climate in which affirmations are the norm rather than the exception. And that is the purpose of the strategies in step three. Turn to page 82 for the affirming exercises.

4 STRETCHING

When a group has moved through the first three steps of community building, they're ready for step four. By the end of step three, group members are working together, sharing ideas, and affirming one another. The comfort level has been established so kids can trust each other enough to move to a new level—a level of discomfort. It's in the uncomfortable circumstances that kids often learn the most.

Stretching activities place students in new and unfamiliar territory, thereby providing personal, individual growth as well as group growth. When fatigued students reach the summit of a seemingly impossible climb and they've done so through the encouragement of friends, they realize they can accomplish anything with Christ and his body of believers. Since, as a group, we can't always go to the mountain, stretching exercises bring the mountain to the group.

Some of these exercises involve physical challenges, some emotional challenges, and some relational challenges. But all provide an opportunity to move beyond the comfort zone and achieve growth in relationships. The stretching exercises begin on page 97.

5 DEEPER SHARING AND GOAL SETTING

With step five, individuals learn to trust the group enough to share their deepest feelings. A youth group at this level offers an environment in which students can express their inner hurts, visions, and struggles without fear of ridicule. Why can they do it here? Because they've built trust through bond building and opening up, they've felt accepted through affirming, and they've worked as a team on a challenge through stretching. Now they're ready to do something they may never have done before.

However, not all of a person's deep thoughts or covert actions are appropriate to share in a group setting. What a student shares Sunday night, he or she may regret having shared Monday morning. Obviously, a student should be discouraged from telling the whole youth group vivid details of his or her sex life. Students should be directed to seek counsel on intimate struggles with you or a counselor.

The strategies for deeper sharing and goal setting, starting on page 116, are structured to make people think about where they need growth (spiritual and otherwise) in their own lives and then share those areas with the group. Often the group will help an individual come up with a game plan to achieve growth in a certain area.

RESULTS

As individuals move through these five steps, they'll become people who listen, share, affirm, and trust. In time, they'll develop habits that allow them to act this way naturally, without the structure you've provided through the activities in this book.

SUGGESTIONS FOR TRUST BUILDING

DETERMINE ACTIVITY TIMES

A general time frame has been suggested for each activity. But these are only suggested times. Watch what's happening with your group and cut or expand the activity time accordingly. But please don't short-circuit the discussion questions. The questions encourage students to reflect on and verbalize what's going on. And through the discussion process, kids discover new ideas and grow from their experiences.

CREATE SMALL GROUPS

An ideal size for small-group sharing is four to seven people. If your youth group is larger than that, you'll want to break it into smaller groups. However, it's not necessary to keep these smaller groups the same week after week. As students experience community building, they can transfer what they've learned from one small group to another.

USE THIS BOOK AS A TOOL

Don't take this book too seriously. It's simply one tool to be used in your ministry to teenagers. Community building is important. It serves as a building block to better teaching and growth. But it's only one part of what you do.

READ YOUR GROUP

Community building is an art, not a science. Don't plan activities this way: "On week one, I'll do bond building. On week two, I'll do some opening-up stuff. On week three, we'll stretch. On week four, we'll move to affirming. And then next month, after community is built, we'll do something else." It's not that simple!

Community building is a lifelong process. You'll always need to affirm kids (and encourage them to affirm each other). Throughout the year, you'll need to continue bond building, opening up, affirming, stretching, and deeper sharing and goal setting—especially as new teenagers join the group.

Although this book separates the steps into neat chapters, community building doesn't always happen in "chapter" order. One caution, however: Don't attempt activities in steps four or five until you've spent some time in the first three steps. Kids who aren't comfortable sharing openly will be easily scared off by activities that require a great deal of trust.

FIND TEACHABLE MOMENTS

Look for teachable moments as your group participates in these community-building activities. A teachable moment occurs when something unexpected happens that could provide a segue into a wonderful discussion and learning time for kids. For example, the moment a youth group member quits a game because he or she thinks it's stupid can be a great opportunity for learning. In that situation you might explore the person's feelings only to discover he or she feels left out. What a great chance for kids to talk about community and express their love and concern!

But remember that teachable moments don't mean you do all the teaching. If you see an opportunity for further exploration, your job is to get the discussion going. Give kids the opportunity to discover their own nuggets of truth as they explore the situation. Guide the discussions only if they veer from a Christian perspective of the issue.

MODIFY ACTIVITIES

The suggestions in this book work just fine as they're written. But you may want to modify them for your own circumstances (or simply to repeat favorite activities without seeming repetitious). For instance, in bond-building exercises you might modify an activity by giving some students an advantage or a handicap such as blindfolds or crutches. Feel free to use these strategies as springboards to your own.

IDENTIFY SENSITIVE ISSUES

Difficult and sensitive issues are bound to surface as you build trust in your group. Be ready to refer students to competent counselors if a key issue such as abuse or depression emerges. Have a list of competent counselors ready and don't be reluctant to refer.

OTHER OPTIONS

Use the exercises with groups other than teenagers. If you're invited to lead an adult function, try some of these exercises with adults. You'll be amazed at how the activities transcend age divisions.

Now that you've got the big picture, let's move on!

CHAPTER 2

BOND
BUILDING

Bond-building activities force teenagers to work together to solve problems. As students work side by side, they learn about themselves and the group in a nonthreatening environment. Unity also begins to develop within the group. These fun, shared experiences break down walls which may separate members of your group. And as the barriers are broken, bonds are built in their place.

The activities in this chapter are effective because they place people in situations that require communication and cooperation to overcome physical and emotional barriers. Your teenagers must work together, sharing their variety of gifts and abilities to solve each puzzle. Each group member becomes a participant in completing the task.

As teenagers work to solve the problem, gregarious, outgoing participants and shy, quiet ones find they have equal contributions to make. Bond-building activities build students' self-esteem as kids overcome obstacles that seemed insurmountable at first. The exercises help individuals see their own strengths as well as their fellow group members' strengths. And the activities become catalysts for deeper sharing by encouraging people to communicate with one another.

To maximize the bond-building experiences, students must share with their peers the insights they've gained. And they must listen to their peers' great ideas, too. The discussion questions help teenagers clarify and cement the lessons they've learned.

HOW TO USE THE BOND-BUILDING EXERCISES

1. Carefully select a bond-building exercise. Read the descriptions, instructions, and questions for the activity. Collect the materials you'll need well in advance of when you'll use them.

2. Be a silent participant. The primary purpose of bond-building activities is *group* interaction. As the leader, you can offer hints and suggestions. But don't take over the decision-making process. Allow group members to make the decisions themselves. And don't try to give students the "right" or "best" answers or solutions. In most cases, it's best for leaders to silently participate in the exercises.

A leader leads best by *doing,* so be involved. And be willing to be the target (see the Water-Balloon Blitz on page 53) as group members try to solve a problem.

3. Be safety conscious. All the exercises in this chapter are safe, but some require the use of "spotters"—people who assist in the prevention of injuries if a participant slips or falls. If the activity suggests spotters, please have more than enough on hand.

4. Use small groups if your overall group is too large for the activity. Form smaller groups if your entire group is larger than the recommended size for the specific exercise. No youth group is too large to do any of the suggested activities. All you need to do is form smaller groups for the events.

5. Offer clear instructions. Give the group clear and specific rules and instructions for the task. Take extra time if necessary so everyone understands. The setup is very important to success. And if *you* don't understand the rules or the setup very well, take plenty of time before leading the activity to walk through the process so you gain a clear understanding.

6. Don't focus on mistakes. In your discussion time, focus on the ultimate success the participants experienced as they worked together to achieve the goals of the exercise.

7. Wait for answers. When you ask a question, give time for a response. Don't be afraid of silence. When students get uncomfortable enough with the silence, they'll most likely respond. By waiting, you show that you genuinely value their opinions, and they'll more readily enter into discussion and benefit from it. One way to practice this skill is to silently count to 15 before saying anything if you don't get an immediate response to a question.

8. Focus on the students' personal experiences and feelings. Once personal feelings are discussed, the philosophical and theological implications of the exercise can come alive. To abbreviate the process and first concentrate on philosophical concepts is to miss the point of bond building.

9. Be sure everyone gets an opportunity to talk. If the group seems reluctant to share, or if a few individuals dominate the conversation, go around the circle and ask each person to respond with his or her feelings. For example, you might ask, "How did you feel, Lisa, as you tried to help the group build the pyramid?" Going around the circle and asking this kind of question can be a non-threatening method of facilitating discussion.

10. Refrain from giving advice. Students need adults who will listen. They reject most pat answers. We can show we care by listening *before* we offer advice. Since bond-building exercises are first and foremost designed to create stronger relationships, giving advice isn't usually appropriate anyway. Indeed, as group members interact and share with one another, they often come up with the same or better solutions than you may have offered as advice.

11. Use the deeper discussion questions later in the overall community-building process. The deeper discussion questions are not designed to be used by a group that is in the first stages of community building. But the questions have been added so you can use the same exercises as a springboard to step two (opening up) or step five (deeper sharing and goal setting).

If your group is moving along in the community-building process and kids have developed relationships that are trusting enough, you can use the deeper discussion questions in these bond-building exercises.

12. Be creative. Modify the activities or write your own questions. You and your other leaders have great creativity, wonderful gifts, and a superb understanding of your own group. So use these exercises the way they've been written or modify them to be even more effective.

Please keep these suggestions in mind as you begin the first step of building community in your youth group. Have fun!

BACK-TO-BACK ART

TIME: 20 minutes.

MATERIALS: several simple pictures (such as a smiley face, a dog, a building, or a boat), pencils or pens, and paper.

GROUP SIZE: five to 15.

BEST FOR: junior or senior high.

DESCRIPTION

Ask everyone to stand in a single-file line facing the same direction then have them sit down.

Explain that the person at the end of the line will be shown a picture. That person will then use his or her finger to draw that picture on the back of the person in front of him or her. The person whose back is drawn on will then draw his or her perception of the picture on the back of the next person. Explain that the goal is to draw as similar a picture to the original picture as possible.

The progression will continue until it reaches the last person in line. The last person will draw the picture on a piece of paper for everyone to see. The final picture will then be compared with the original.

Try this exercise with several different pictures and let people switch places so they can see what it's like being at the beginning, middle, and end of the line.

DISCUSSION

● How did you feel about your performance in this activity? Explain.

● What made it difficult to come up with an accurate duplication of the original picture?

● In what ways did you work together as a team to accomplish this task?

● What could you have done to improve your performance?

TEACHABLE MOMENT

Back-to-Back Art helps the participants focus on teamwork and, more specifically, communication within a team. This exercise highlights the difficulty of communicating and the real possibilities for misunderstanding and miscommunication within a group.

DEEPER DISCUSSION

● Whose fault was it that the picture got distorted? Is it important to find fault before you can solve a problem? Why or why not?

● Which was easier: drawing the picture on someone's back or trying to determine what was being drawn on yours? Explain.

● What were the keys to communicating and understanding the picture? What are the keys to communicating and understanding people every day?

● Tell about a time recently when you felt misunderstood. How did it happen? How did you feel? How did you resolve this misunderstanding?

● What are specific steps you can take toward being better understood by your friends and family? How can you improve your ability to understand your friends and family?

BLIND CONSTRUCTION

TIME: 20 minutes.

MATERIALS: building materials (snow, sand, building blocks, rope, bricks, boxes—you choose!) and one blindfold for each participant.

GROUP SIZE: five per construction group.

BEST FOR: junior and senior high.

DESCRIPTION

Choose your building materials based on available resources. Make sure that you have a large enough room and enough materials so that everyone in the group can participate in the construction. You may choose to do this activity outside, weather and location permitting.

Show the group members their construction materials and then blindfold them.

Once they're blindfolded, describe the structure the group members are to build and let them go to it. Structures can be anything from a wooden box to a snow fort. Choose something large enough that each participant can have a role in creating it.

Have the group members decide when they've completed the task. Resist the temptation to help them during the activity.

Station spotters around the work area to keep kids out of danger from the tools or environment.

By simply changing the conditions, you can repeat this activity. For example, you can let kids draw a picture of the structure they're supposed to build before you blindfold them. Or you can have them construct it without the blindfolds before trying it with the blindfolds.

DISCUSSION

- How high was your frustration level on this exercise? Explain.

- How pleased were you with your final results? Explain.

- What did you learn about the importance of sight and communication in this exercise?

TEACHABLE MOMENT

This exercise focuses on the aspects of teamwork, communication, and sight. Team members will compensate for their "handicap" by working harder together to complete the project.

DEEPER DISCUSSION

● What was one of the most frustrating projects you've ever undertaken? What happened? How could a team have helped you in that situation?

● In this exercise, when you and your group had a handicap—lack of sight—what did you do to compensate for it to finish the project?

● What sort of compensation skills do you use in life to overcome your weaknesses? How well do they work?

● In what ways do you feel "blind" in life? How frustrating is it for you to operate in these blind areas? Explain.

BLIND FACE-PAINTING

TIME:	30 minutes.
MATERIALS:	blindfolds, paintbrushes, face paints, and awards (optional).
GROUP SIZE:	any number.
BEST FOR:	junior and senior high.

DESCRIPTION

Ask everyone to select a partner and explain that they're going to do some face-painting. Encourage partners to discuss what designs they want painted on their faces.

Then blindfold the kids who will be painting first.

Emphasize that the person being painted must help his or her blindfolded partner by giving painting instructions. Also explain that the person painting will soon be painted. This will prevent kids from getting out of hand with their painting.

After teenagers finish painting their partners' faces, have them switch roles.

When everyone's been painted, give awards for such things as the best use of color, the messiest face, and the most hair painted. Make up enough fun awards that each pair gets one.

Then, as a finale to the face-painting, blindfold the whole group and let them contribute to a masterpiece on your face and the faces of other youth workers or sponsors.

DISCUSSION

● When you were the person being painted, how difficult was it to give instructions to the artist? Explain.

● How did you feel when you were being painted? when you were the painter?

● How did you feel about the final product?

TEACHABLE MOMENT

This exercise focuses on teamwork, communication, and artistic gifts. It also helps remind the students that "what goes around comes around" and that what they do affects other people.

DEEPER DISCUSSION

● How much did you appreciate your partner painting your face? What things in life do you hate "having done to you"? How do you deal with these kinds of issues in your life?

● Obviously, you had an impact on someone's face when you were painting it. What are some other ways that your actions impact people in real life? How aware of the consequences of your actions on others are you?

● What did you learn about communication from this exercise? How did your partner help you with his or her verbal instructions?

● What insights can you transfer from this exercise to life? How can you apply these in your day-to-day communication?

CONVOY

TIME: 20 minutes.

MATERIALS: Bibles; two-by-fours; plywood; hammers; nails; rope; and skateboards, shopping carts, and anything else that moves on wheels.

GROUP SIZE: 10 to 20.

BEST FOR: senior high.

DESCRIPTION

Gather in an empty parking lot. Designate a starting line and finish line for a brief race. It's best to have the finish at the end of a slight downhill grade and about 15 to 20 yards from the starting point—longer if you want to make the activity tougher.

Explain to the group that they must move on wheels as a connected unit from the start to the finish line. First, the group must construct a vehicle with the resources you've given that can transport them the given distance.

No one in the group is allowed to touch the ground between the start and finish lines except two people designated as "motors." The job of the motors is to push or pull the vehicle loaded down with people to the finish line.

Depending on your available resources, the creation of the vehicle could be quite a challenge for kids. Encourage teenagers to be creative in making their vehicle. For instance, two people standing on a skateboard holding onto a rope connecting them with another vehicle is a great solution to a vehicle that's too small.

If the vehicle comes apart in mid-journey, kids must return to the starting line and try again.

Supervise the construction and journey closely to ensure safety.

DISCUSSION

- What kind of leadership was required to ensure success?
- What was your level of participation in this activity? Explain.
- What did you learn from this activity?

TEACHABLE MOMENT

This activity focuses on the importance of teamwork; problem solving; persistence; and members' individual gifts, such as leadership, design ability, and strength.

DEEPER DISCUSSION

● What roles, gifts, and talents were needed in this activity to accomplish the goals?

● What role did you take? What specific contribution did you make to the total effort?

● Read 1 Corinthians 12:4-31. How do you see individual talents and roles at work in life? How is what happened in this activity similar to what should happen in your group and the church?

DOTS

TIME: 20 minutes.

MATERIALS: yarn or string.

GROUP SIZE: 10 or more.

BEST FOR: junior and senior high.

DESCRIPTION

Assign nine people to be "dots." These nine people can include youth sponsors. Have the dots sit on the floor forming a square with three dots per side and one dot in the middle. It is important that the dots are evenly spaced so that connecting three dots in a row will form a straight line. The rest of the group will be the puzzle solvers.

O   O   O

O   O   O

O   O   O

If your group is smaller than 10, use chairs as the dots and have all the kids act as puzzle solvers.

Tell the puzzle solvers that their goal is to connect all nine dots using four straight lines created with one continuous piece of yarn or string. If anyone has seen this puzzle before and knows the solution, ask him or her not to give it away.

Allow individual volunteers a chance to solve the puzzle first but don't allow any communication between the individual and other puzzle solvers or the dots.

If no one figures out the puzzle individually, allow the puzzle solvers to work as a group. Encourage puzzle solvers to get advice from the dots, too.

If they still can't figure it out, show kids the solution as shown on page 29.

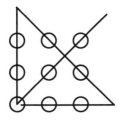 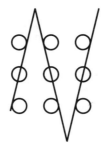

DISCUSSION

- How successful was your group at figuring out this puzzle? Was the puzzle solved in a reasonable amount of time? Why or why not?

- What were keys to success in this activity?

- What did you learn from doing this?

TEACHABLE MOMENT

This activity focuses on creativity, the concept of "drawing outside the lines," teamwork, going it alone or as a team, and group dynamics.

DEEPER DISCUSSION

- The solution to this problem is based on seeing a situation somewhat differently than how we normally perceive things. It also involves "moving outside the lines." How much do you "color outside the lines" in your everyday life? Explain.

- On a scale of 1 to 10 with 1 being spontaneous and 10 being rigid, where would you place yourself in relation to how you live your life? Explain.

- What did you learn about the role of individuals and the role of the group in problem solving?

- What's a problem you're working on now where you could use the problem-solving skills of a group?

EGG DROP

TIME: 20 minutes.

MATERIALS: Bibles, paper cups, eggs, plastic bags or towels, and paper towels.

GROUP SIZE: two or more.

BEST FOR: senior high.

DESCRIPTION

Have teenagers each choose a partner. Give each pair a paper cup, two eggs, and a plastic bag or towel.

Have one partner in each pair lie face up with a plastic bag or towel under his or her head and a paper cup placed on his or her forehead. Participants can hold the paper cups in place with their hands.

Explain to the other partners that the task is to crack an egg into the strategically placed paper cups while standing directly above their teammates. Make sure the students who get the first crack know that they will also have a turn on the floor.

After the first egg is dropped have the partners trade places and repeat the exercise. If you have a large group, half of the kids can get on the floor at the same time for a simultaneous egg drop. If you have a smaller group, it's more fun to do one egg drop at a time in front of everyone.

You might want to do this at a retreat breakfast and collect the eggs that land in cups for a scrambled-egg breakfast. If you prefer, you can substitute water-soaked sponges for the eggs. In this case, the object is to squeeze all the water into the cups.

DISCUSSION

- What was it like being the person on the floor?

- What was it like being the person dropping the egg?

- Which position did you like better? Explain.

TEACHABLE MOMENT

This activity forces the students into a situation in which they must trust each other. It can lead to a discussion of the difficulty of trusting friends, family members, or God.

DEEPER DISCUSSION

● Did you find it difficult to trust your partner when he or she dropped the egg on your face? Why or why not?

● What are the most difficult things in life to trust your friends with?

● Who do you trust more than anyone else? Why?

● How did it feel when you got egg dropped on your face? What are ways your trust has been violated in life?

● As the egg dropper, what was it like to have the person below you at your mercy? Have you ever felt like you were in that kind of position of power in real life? What happened? Were you trustworthy?

● How trustworthy are you with people's thoughts and feelings? How can you become even more trustworthy?

● What are everyday situations in which you're forced to trust others? Is it easy or difficult for you to trust in those situations? Explain.

● Read Proverbs 3:5-6. How is the way we trust others like or unlike the way we should trust God?

GLOVES AND BLINDFOLDS

TIME:	40 minutes.
MATERIALS:	Bibles, one blindfold and one pair of gloves for each participant, and various discretionary supplies.
GROUP SIZE:	six to 16.
BEST FOR:	junior and senior high.

DESCRIPTION

Have all but two students put on blindfolds and gloves. This activity works best if different types of gloves—such as old work gloves, surgical gloves, rubber gloves, and winter gloves—are distributed. To add even more variety, have some teenagers wear mismatched pairs such as a work glove on the right hand and a surgical glove on the left.

Explain to the group that the only two people allowed to speak are the two who have not been blindfolded. In advance of the activity, instruct one of the two sighted people to deliberately give instructions that contradict the instructions of the other person. This subterfuge should not be obvious.

For the next 20 minutes, have the sighted kids lead the group in performing an activity that requires some fine motor skills. Examples of this kind of activity are making a pizza from scratch, playing Monopoly, setting up dominoes in an intricate design, making a church banner, and building a castle out of blocks.

DISCUSSION

● How were you handicapped in this activity?

● What frustrated you the most about this activity? (At this time explain that you had secretly instructed one of the sighted people to give confusing directions.)

● How is the way you received varying messages from the two sighted people like the way you receive messages from others in everyday life?

● What did you learn about teamwork from this exercise?

TEACHABLE MOMENT

Students will better understand what it means to be limited physically and to depend upon one another to succeed.

DEEPER DISCUSSION

● Did you feel your handicap was greater than others' because of the kind of gloves you wore? How did that make you feel?

● Did you feel that the instructions you were given were clear? Why or why not?

● In life what do you feel are your handicaps? How do they impact you? How have others helped you rise above your handicaps?

● How sensitive are you to others' physical, mental, and emotional handicaps? How do you think you could become more sensitive?

● Read Matthew 9:18-38. What does this passage tell us about the way Jesus related to people who had physical, mental, and emotional handicaps? What can we learn from Jesus' example?

HEE HAW

TIME:	20 minutes.
MATERIALS:	Bibles.
GROUP SIZE:	10 or more (an even number).
BEST FOR:	junior and senior high.

DESCRIPTION

Have an even number of people stand in a circle facing the middle with their shoulders almost touching.

Ask group members to count off around the circle. But instead of counting one, two, one, two, have them count hee, haw, hee, haw. There should be an even number of "Hees" and "Haws."

Ask everyone in the circle to join hands. Explain that when you yell "go," all of the Hees should lean forward and all of the Haws should, at the same time, lean back. As they do this, they should shout out their titles—"Hee" or "Haw." Then when you yell "go" again, the Hees should lean backward and the Haws forward and shout their titles.

Stress that they're not allowed to move their feet and that they need to keep a firm grip on one another's hands. If one link in the circle gives way the whole circle will follow. As they practice this exercise, they should be able to lean far forward and backward without the circle collapsing.

When the group perfects its leaning skills, have its members lean in and out in rhythm. As the "caller" you will determine when they change directions.

DISCUSSION

● How reluctant were you to lean in and out when this activity started? Did your confidence increase at all as the exercise progressed? Why or why not?

● What was the key to success in this activity?

● What else did you learn from this activity?

TEACHABLE MOMENT

This activity focuses on trust, on the importance of each person playing his or her role, on cooperation, and on the success that follows when people trust each other and do what they need to do.

DEEPER DISCUSSION

● What part did trust play in this activity?

● What would have happened if just one person had "hee'd" when he or she should have "haw'd"?

● How is the way you all worked together (or didn't work together) like real life?

● How important did you *feel* in your role as a Hee or a Haw? How important were you really, regardless of how you felt? Explain.

● Read 1 John 4:7-12. What does this passage tell us about the way God values us?

IMPROVISATION THEATER

TIME: 30 minutes.

MATERIALS: Bibles, slips of paper, a pencil, and two containers.

GROUP SIZE: four to six per small group.

BEST FOR: senior high.

PREPARATION: Before the meeting develop a list of character types and locations for the improvisations. Here are a few ideas:

Character Types	Locations
astronauts	bowling alley
surfers	California beach
rock stars	Disneyland
athletes	Mars
cartoon characters	ski slopes

Write each item on a separate slip of paper. Place the character slips and location slips in two different containers.

DESCRIPTION

Improvisational presentations are fun, spontaneous, and great opportunities for people to work together as a team.

● The idea of improvisation is to be spontaneous. Teams should not know the subject of their presentations until they get up to perform them.

● Once groups are called forward, each should be assigned a character type and a location that don't necessarily fit together. For example, astronauts at a bowling alley or plumbers at a political convention.

● In this form of improvisation, kids form pairs within their groups. Each pair works as a team. One person is the character, who talks and reacts, and the other person is the character's manipulator, who initiates all the movements of the character. The manipulator stands behind the character and moves the character's arms, legs, head, and anything else that needs to be moved. The character cannot move without the guidance of the manipulator but the character *is* free to talk. The manipulator *can't* talk.

Explain the activity. One at a time, call each group forward to choose a character type and location from separate containers. Give group members two or three minutes to discuss among themselves what they plan to act out. Then have a volunteer introduce the group's characters and describe the scene.

Allow five to seven minutes for each group to present its improvisation. Don't let improvisations go too long. If it seems the group is struggling, call time and move on to the next group.

DISCUSSION

- How hard was it to perform in front of the group? Explain.

- How did your teammates help or hinder you in performing?

- Is it easier to be the manipulator or the character? Explain.

- How are these two roles like roles people play in everyday life?

TEACHABLE MOMENT

This activity gives participants a chance to overcome what might be for some a difficult challenge: performing under pressure. Consider discussing the roles of spontaneity, teamwork, pressure, and different personality types in this activity.

DEEPER DISCUSSION

- When do you feel like you're "on stage" in life? What roles do you most often play? What is one of the hardest roles for you to accept in life? one of the easiest? How would you rate your performance in these roles?

- How spontaneous are you? Do you wish you were more or less spontaneous? Explain.

- When do you feel the greatest pressure to perform? How does that make you feel?

- How do your "teammates" in life help you in the roles you play? Read Psalm 139:7-12 and Matthew 19:26. How can God help you when you're forced into a difficult role?

LEAN ON ME

TIME:	15 minutes.
MATERIALS:	Bibles.
GROUP SIZE:	any number.
BEST FOR:	junior and senior high.

DESCRIPTION

Have kids each find a partner and stand a little more than an arm's length apart facing each other.

Instruct teenagers to stretch their arms out in front of them with their palms facing forward. While keeping their bodies as straight as possible and their feet in place, they are to fall forward, catching each other by the palms of their hands. Have pairs hold that position for a while and then push off so they return to the standing position.

Next, have everyone take a step back and try it again. Keep moving partners back until they can't successfully complete the activity.

When the group gets good at this, have all the pairs line up together shoulder to shoulder facing their partners.

Have one side take a half step to the left so the two lines facing each other are staggered.

Have kids each lean toward one another simultaneously, using one hand to support their partner and one hand to support the person next to their partner. In this configuration all but two of the kids are supported by two people. Assign one person to anchor each end by using both hands to support one hand of the person opposite.

See how far apart the two lines can get while successfully leaning on each other and then returning to a vertical position.

DISCUSSION

- What made this activity succeed?

- How did you feel as you moved farther apart from your partner?

- What else did you learn from this activity?

TEACHABLE MOMENT

The kids will be forced to support one another, rely on one another, and trust one another.

DEEPER DISCUSSION

- How was it different when you had two people helping you as opposed to only one?

- Who are the key people in your life who help you stand up and spring back when you fall?

- Read Ecclesiastes 4:9-12 and talk about the importance of having friends help each other face the pangs of loneliness and the threat of attack. When have friends provided you with what the writer of Ecclesiastes describes in this passage?

MEAL MADNESS

DESCRIPTION

Gather group members around a table or tables and ask them to sit down. Introduce the food preparers and explain that they've prepared a true feast.

Have your adult volunteers assist you in tying kids' wrists together (one person's right wrist is tied to his or her neighbor's left wrist, and so on around the table). Make sure kids' hands are tied in such a way that there can be little movement by one person without affecting his or her neighbor.

Keep this wrist-tying plan a surprise. If kids know they're going to have their wrists tied, the activity will lose its impact and you may lose a few students.

Place in the middle of the table an equal number of forks, spoons, and knives totaling the number of people around the table (one utensil for each person). For example, if you have 15 students, you would have five forks, five spoons, and five knives in the middle of the table. Tell the hungry teenagers they can distribute the utensils any way they want, but that at all times each person can only be holding one utensil.

If possible, have an adult volunteer tie you into the group, too. Then have the food preparers bring the meal in course by course and enjoy!

DISCUSSION

- What did you like about this experience? What did you dislike? Explain.

- What are three lessons you learned from this activity?

- How was this meal like or unlike a family dinner at your home?

TEACHABLE MOMENT

The group will learn about teamwork, serving one another, being connected with and relying on others, and being limited by rules and resources beyond their control.

DEEPER DISCUSSION

- How did you feel being connected in this exercise? How is that like the way you feel connected to others in life? Are there people in your life you feel you should be more connected to but aren't? Who are they? Why do you think you should be more connected?

- What did you learn about being a servant in this activity? How can you apply that lesson to life?

- Read Matthew 25:31-46. How does this message apply to the activity we just experienced? How does it apply to our daily lives?

- Do you sometimes feel too tied to people? If so, explain. What would you like to do to get untied from them?

- Read Romans 12:4-8. How is the way we worked together in the meal like the way we should work together as Christian brothers and sisters?

O BSTACLE OLYMPICS

TIME: 30 minutes.

MATERIALS: Bibles, paper slips, pencil, cloth strips for tying and blindfolding, wheelchairs, and crutches.

GROUP SIZE: 10 to 20.

BEST FOR: junior and senior high.

PREPARATION: Set up an obstacle course before the meeting. Set clear boundaries so participants can't cheat by going around the obstacles without completing the task at hand. The point is to create a situation that causes group members to rely on one another. A jungle gym or a ropes course, tires, a wall to scale, a balance beam to walk across, and something to crawl under are all good elements to use. Use your creativity to create a course that will challenge kids.

Prepare slips of paper naming disabilities such as blindness, paralysis, loss of a leg, loss of the ability to speak, and loss of an arm. You might list more than one disability on some slips.

Read through the activity and try out the obstacle course with adult volunteers before having kids complete it.

DESCRIPTION

Give each person a slip of paper naming a disability. Explain to kids the following limitations for each disability: those who are blind must wear blindfolds; those who are paralyzed must ride in wheelchairs; those who have lost a leg must each bend one leg back, tie it up, and use crutches to walk; those who have lost the ability to speak can't talk from the moment they're assigned the disability until the activity is over; and those who have lost an arm must each tie one arm up in a mock sling.

Explain that this activity will involve completing an obstacle course but that the goal is not to win but to simply finish with the assistance of others. For example, blind participants may need help from people in wheelchairs to stay on course, and people in wheelchairs may need help from blind participants to get over some obstacles. Remind kids they'll need to rely on each other and be reliable. Remember, the goal is for everyone to get through the obstacle course, not to set a speed record.

Explain the course so that kids understand what they have to do and then let them go at it.

Although some teenagers will be skeptical about making it through the course, assure everyone that it is possible. Allow kids to figure out that the blind people can carry the paralyzed people, the paralyzed people can tell the blind people where to go, the one-armed people can support the one-legged people, and so on.

Assign spotters to ensure safety and to provide encouragement and support when needed.

DISCUSSION

● When this activity was first announced and you heard of your disability, did you think you would make it through the course? Why or why not?

● How did you feel when you thought about the task ahead of you? How is that like the way you feel when you're facing significant obstacles in life?

● What surprised you most about this activity?

TEACHABLE MOMENT

This activity helps kids explore what it's like to deal with disabilities. And it helps them learn to rely on people, ask people for help, give help to others, admit shortcomings, admit need, and discover the importance of gifts within the body of Christ.

DEEPER DISCUSSION

● In this activity, how did you help others, and how were you helped?

● What similarities can you see between what happened in the activity and what happens in life?

● How tough was it for you to ask for help in this game? in life?

● How willing were you to help others in this game? in life?

● Read 1 Corinthians 1:10. How does this passage apply to the way we needed to work together in this activity? How does it relate to the way we need to operate in the body of Christ?

RIDDLES

TIME: 20 minutes.

MATERIALS: Bibles, six drinking glasses, water, 3×5 cards, and scissors.

GROUP SIZE: six.

BEST FOR: junior and senior high.

DESCRIPTION

This activity involves the group in solving two riddles. If you have more than six kids in your group, form multiple groups and provide enough materials for each group to work on each riddle at the same time.

Riddle #1: Give six people each a drinking glass and have them stand in a row shoulder to shoulder.

Number the six participants from 1 to 6 (left to right) and fill the glasses of #3, #4, and #5 with water.

Say: **Your challenge is to rearrange yourselves so your glasses alternate as follows from left to right: full, empty, full, empty, full, empty. But only one person in the group of six is allowed to move.**

Give groups time to solve the riddle. If they aren't able to solve it, tell them the solution: Empty the contents of glass #4 into glass #1.

Riddle #2: Give each group several 3×5 cards and a couple of pairs of scissors. Say: **Your task is to cut a hole in the card and have every member squeeze through the hole.**

Give no further instructions and let groups attempt to solve the riddle. If they give up, tell them the solution: Fold the card lengthwise down the middle and stagger cuts that alternate from the folded side to the open side as shown below. The closer the cuts, the larger the hole will be. Cut the fold except for the two end pieces. Carefully unfold it, and the hole will appear.

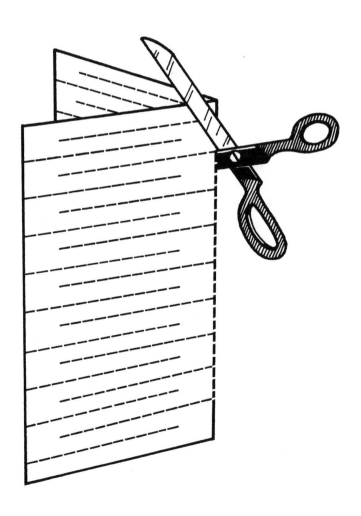

DISCUSSION

- Did you feel like you were a participant or an observer in finding these solutions? Explain.

- What was most difficult about solving these riddles? What was easiest?

- How did you work together to solve the puzzle?

TEACHABLE MOMENT

The activity involves teenagers in creativity, group problem solving, and teamwork.

DEEPER DISCUSSION

- What did it take to solve the riddles? What can help us solve difficult riddles like these?

- How did you feel when you discovered the solution to the riddles? How is that like the way you feel when you discover the answer to a riddle in your life?

- What are riddles in your life right now? What experiences, events, and thoughts are you trying to get a handle on?

- Read Jeremiah 32:27 and Isaiah 40:28-29. How can God help you with the riddles in your life? How can this group help you?

SHEET VOLLEYBALL

| **TIME:** | 25 minutes. |

| **MATERIALS:** | Bibles, two large sheets (or blankets) that may get wet or torn, 25 medium-sized water balloons, a volleyball net, and towels for drying off. |

| **GROUP SIZE:** | eight to 16. |

| **BEST FOR:** | junior and senior high. |

DESCRIPTION

You probably will want to do this activity outside since it involves water balloons. Form two equal-sized teams and assign them to either side of the volleyball net. If you have more than 16 kids, consider having multiple games going at the same time or having kids rotate in and out of one game.

Give each team a sheet and instruct kids to space themselves evenly around it and grab the edge tightly.

Explain the rules of the game. Say: **The object of the game is to see how many times the teams can toss a balloon back and forth without breaking it. You may not catch the balloon with your hands, in your shirts, or with anything other than the sheet.**

After players get the hang of the game, have them play with more than one balloon at a time or with smaller sheets or pillowcases so that each team uses more than one sheet at a time. Play for about 15 minutes or until you run out of water balloons.

DISCUSSION

- What made this game difficult for you? for your team?

- Did you improve in tossing and catching the balloons as the game went along? Why or why not?

- What leadership skills helped keep your team organized?

- What did you learn about working together in this activity?

TEACHABLE MOMENT

This game forces teenagers to work together as a team. They see the benefits of teamwork and the problems that arise when team members don't cooperate. Teenagers also see the importance of team leadership in the success of a group.

DEEPER DISCUSSION

● What are the characteristics of an effective team?

● What benefits are there in being part of a team in everyday life?

● What "teams" do you work with in life? How successful are those teams in accomplishing their goals? Explain.

● Read Ephesians 4:11-12. What are the roles people play in God's community, the church? What roles do you play?

TWISTED

TIME:	20 minutes.
MATERIALS:	Bibles.
GROUP SIZE:	six or more per group.
BEST FOR:	junior and senior high.

DESCRIPTION

Arrange kids in equal, single-file lines of no more than six facing the leader. (At least two lines are needed.)

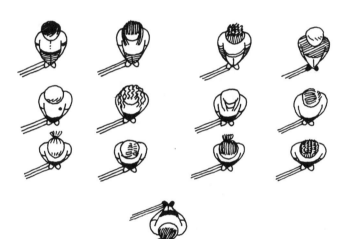

Give instructions similar to these:

● **All who didn't take a shower today, grab the left knee of the person in front of you.**

● **All who've ever had an upset stomach during a test, grab the right elbow of the person directly to your left.**

● **All who like basketball more than baseball, grab the right ear of the person behind you.**

● **All who prefer pizza with pepperoni to pizza with green peppers, grab the left ankle of the person to your right.**

Create your own "twister" statements that relate directly to your youth group. Here are a few more ideas to mix and match:

All who...

    are wearing sneakers

    flunked math

    love cartoons

flossed their teeth today

have been to a foreign country

broke a fingernail within the last week

grab...

the ankle of the person behind you

the back of the neck of the person in front of you

the sole of the shoe of the person to your right.

Kids will eventually run out of hands to grab with. That's okay. When kids are tied in knots, have them try to disentangle themselves without dropping their hands.

Make sure that group members don't grab each other inappropriately. And let people know ahead of time to dress appropriately for the occasion (no skirts or dresses).

For variety, tell kids they can't talk while they attempt to untangle themselves. Or have kids choose one person to act as the director of the untangling and allow only the director to talk.

DISCUSSION

● What did you learn from this exercise?

● What problems did you have getting untangled?

● How did you solve those problems?

● How did you feel during this activity? How is that like the way you feel when you're tangled up with something in everyday life?

TEACHABLE MOMENT

This activity stresses closeness, teamwork, and creativity in solving a problem.

DEEPER DISCUSSION

● What leadership skills were most effective in getting people untangled?

● What tangles you up in life? How do you get free?

● How can your friends help you get untangled from tough situations?

● Read Romans 5:1-11. These verses call God our friend. How is the commitment described in this passage like the commitment we should have toward one another? What responsibility do we have to help others get untangled from tough situations?

UNDER THE FENCE

TIME:	25 minutes.
MATERIALS:	Bibles, 15-foot piece of string and, masking tape.
GROUP SIZE:	five to 10.
BEST FOR:	senior high.

DESCRIPTION

Attach the ends of a 15-foot-long string to two chairs and spread the chairs out as far as possible. The string should be 2 feet off the ground.

Then use masking tape to mark off a 3-foot-wide zone on either side of the string.

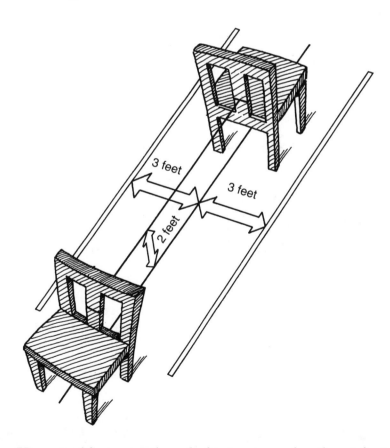

Say: **Your goal is to get the whole group under the string without touching it. You cannot use the chairs on either side of the string as supports, and in the taped-off zone your feet**

are the only things that can touch the ground. If someone touches the string with any part of his or her body or touches the ground in the taped-off zone with anything other than his or her feet, that person must try again. Once a person has gone under the string, he or she can't go back on the other side to help.

This activity may prove to be too difficult for your group. If so, consider moving the string up to 2½ feet above the ground. Or consider allowing one person to break the "feet only" rule in the taped-off zone.

Some kids may be able to limbo under the string, but the majority will have to figure out a way to get under the string with the help of other group members.

Encourage kids to be creative.

DISCUSSION

- What was most difficult about this exercise? What was easiest?

- What examples of teamwork did you observe during this activity?

- What did you learn about working together in this activity?

TEACHABLE MOMENT

This activity stresses cooperation and the importance of different roles in the successful completion of a task.

DEEPER DISCUSSION

- What was your role in getting the group under the string?

- How did you feel about your contribution to the success of the group?

- How did you feel when you first heard what the task was? When have you had a similar feeling about a task in everyday life? What have you learned from this activity that you can apply to the difficult tasks you face in daily life?

- Read Romans 12:3-8. How does this passage relate to this exercise?

Note: To enhance this activity, first do the "Electric Fence" activity on page 37 of *Building Community in Youth Groups* (Group Publishing). Then lead this activity. Have kids discuss the similarities and differences between the two activities.

WATER-BALLOON BLITZ

TIME: 20 minutes.

MATERIALS: Bibles, rope, a large playing field, and lots of water balloons.

GROUP SIZE: 10 to 15.

BEST FOR: junior and senior high.

PREPARATION: Use rope to make a small circle (about 10 feet in diameter) in the center of a playing field. Then use another rope to make a larger circle (about 20 feet in diameter) encircling the smaller circle.

DESCRIPTION

Choose a volunteer to be the target. The target will stand in the inner circle and may not leave that circle. Ask three or four volunteers to be the water-balloon launchers. They'll stand outside the outer circle and attempt to soak the target with water balloons. The remaining group members will be the protectors. The protectors will stand in the ring formed by the two circles and attempt to keep the water balloons from soaking the target. They can do this by deflecting, absorbing, catching, and blocking the water balloons. Their only limitation is that they cannot go inside the target's circle or outside the larger circle.

Play the game until 20 or 30 balloons have been tossed. Then have kids repeat the game playing different roles. When everyone is soaked, it's probably a good time to end the game.

DISCUSSION

● How did you feel about the role you were assigned? How did you feel about changing roles after the first round of the game?

● Which role did you prefer? Explain.

● What did you learn from the roles you played that you can apply to daily life?

TEACHABLE MOMENT

This activity focuses on sacrifice, service, loyalty, and putting people down.

DEEPER DISCUSSION

● What might each of the three roles (target, launcher, and protector) compare to in your life?

● Of the three roles, which do you play most in life? Explain.

● Who are you currently "protecting" in life? Why? How do you feel about this role?

● What kinds of "water balloons" do we launch at our friends? our family members? people we don't get along with? How can we change our actions so we don't drench people with negative words or actions?

● Read Romans 12:14-21. How do these verses apply to how we should treat each other?

Most teenagers will talk openly about themselves only when they feel *comfortable and accepted in a group*. However, in many areas of their lives, teenagers *don't* feel comfortable and accepted. And so they aren't used to sharing.

When a group cares enough to listen intently, a sense of unity is built, friendships develop, barriers break down, and community develops.

The opening-up exercises help students *begin* to express their ideas and feelings. And the more a person shares, the more he or she discovers new insights about God, self, and others. That's the purpose of the exercises in this chapter.

Two things must happen for students to move through this second step of community building. First, kids must learn to risk. Second, the group must learn to *respond* appropriately.

If a teenager risks and then is laughed at or rebuffed, he or she may lose trust in the group. It may be a long time (or never) before that person opens up again. But if group members respond positively and with caring concern, the teenager develops confidence in the group and will probably gain respect for and trust in the group.

Teenagers have been taught by experience to protect themselves and be on guard. The opening-up strategies are designed to let students test the waters of sharing in a nonthreatening way.

HOW TO USE THE OPENING-UP EXERCISES

1. Talk to your teenagers about the need to listen. Before you begin the opening-up exercises, remind teenagers to listen as intently as possible to the person sharing. Ask them to be encouraging and responsive. Remind kids that listening means more than sitting quietly. Help kids understand that active listening means making eye contact, nodding their heads in agreement, and focusing on what's being said (not on what they think is going to be said).

Encourage kids to ask clarifying questions such as "I don't quite understand; could you explain that a bit more?" or "I'm interested; could you tell me a little more?"

CHAPTER

3

OPENING
UP

And don't forget to personally model good listening skills as *you* minister to youth.

2. Accept rather than confront. Don't use opening-up exercises as teachable moments to instruct and correct. Remember the purpose of these activities: to help students *begin* to share in a safe environment. Instruction and correction will come later. When students share from their hearts, they need to experience acceptance first. At this second stage in community building, confrontation can be too threatening and can short-circuit your goals.

3. Discourage tangential discussions based on something a teenager shares. Encourage teenagers to share by asking clarifying questions but don't get off the subject and spend lots of time on discussions that put the sharer on the spot.

4. Thank each person when he or she finishes sharing. This is not only common courtesy, but it also provides positive feedback and affirmation and encourages the student to share again.

5. Model openness as a leader. A good leader shares first. Why? To prove that he or she is the leader? No. The leader's response establishes the level of vulnerability and openness for the whole group. If your response to an opening-up activity is purely superficial, the rest of the group's responses will probably be superficial, too.

Be willing to allow the youth to see some of your imperfections. The teenagers will see by your honesty and openness that you don't have to be perfect to be loved and used by God.

6. Facilitate the process of sharing. If your group is not used to sharing, you may want to ask a question and then go around the circle and ask everyone to participate. Make it clear, however, that anyone can choose not to share.

7. Use small groups. The optimum group size for all these exercises is four to seven people. A larger group will slow down sharing and cause some participants to feel intimidated and overwhelmed. Large groups should be split into smaller ones. (The estimated times for these activities are calculated for groups of seven people.) If you have several leaders in your youth group, you may want to disperse them among the smaller groups.

8. Be aware of the differing vulnerability levels in your group. Vulnerability can be defined as openness—the willingness to risk, to share even to the point of being misunderstood or hurt. For these exercises to be effective, you need to be sure you don't move beyond what the group can handle. Examine the vulnerability level listed for each exercise and think through the questions in light of where your group is in the community-building process. Imagine how individuals in your group might handle the activity. Then select exercises your group can handle.

Don't be *too* cautious or hesitant. Young people are often willing to be more open than we think. If you've spent time on the bond-building exercises and carefully followed the previous suggestions, all of these exercises should work well to help build community in your youth group.

CASTING CALL

TIME: 30 minutes.

MATERIALS: newsprint and marker or chalkboard and chalk.

VULNERABILITY: moderate.

DESCRIPTION

Gather the group together and have them sit facing you.

Sit in a chair facing the group and explain that you're the director of a soon-to-be-released major motion picture and you're casting parts for the film. Explain that everyone in the group will have a starring role in the movie.

Tell kids that they're going to get to choose the characters they'll play. Kids can either choose from a list you'll provide or come up with their own characters. The only requirement is that teenagers have to explain the reasons for their choices and the similarities between their characters and themselves.

Print the following list on newsprint or a blackboard and ask teenagers each to choose a character from the list. Remind kids that they can create their own roles instead.

the man in the white hat	the race-car driver
the woman in white	the computer genius
the villain	the patriot
the detective	the gangster
the comedian	the parent
the rock star	the spoiled brat
the surfer	the loner
the socialite	the Reverend
the sidekick	the mysterious stranger
the fashion plate	the business executive
the teacher	the cop
the jock	the adventurer
the rebel	the artist
the nerd	the servant

One at a time, have volunteers share their answers to the first discussion question. Then have the whole group (or small groups) discuss the other questions.

DISCUSSION

● Which character did you select? How is that character like or unlike you in real life?

● If the movie were going to be about our youth group, what would be a good title for the film? Explain.

● Which character was chosen most often? Why was that character chosen more than any other?

● What did you learn about yourself and the group from this activity?

CHILDHOOD MEMORIES

TIME: 45 minutes.

MATERIALS: balls and snacks.

VULNERABILITY: low.

DESCRIPTION

This series of activities helps students remember their childhood.

Gather the group together and explain that everyone gets to be a child again. Establish the following rules to help kids get into being children again.

● When you raise your hand, it means "Quiet, please" and everyone in the group must immediately be quiet and raise their hands, too.

● If anyone in the group is out of line during the activities and discussions, he or she must take a "time out" and sit in a corner. (This is meant for fun, not discipline.)

Organize and play some of the following children's games. If you're unfamiliar with the rules, have kids help you make up new ones.

● Duck, Duck, Goose
● Dodge Ball
● Red Rover
● Freeze Tag
● Capture the Flag
● Kick the Can
● Hide-and-Seek

After the games explain that it's snack time. Give kids childhood snacks such as Twinkies, fruit pies, and cookies and milk.

If your group is larger than eight, form small groups according to the kind of snack kids chose. For example, have all the people who chose Twinkies get together in a small circle and have all the people who chose fruit pies form another circle. Make sure there are no more than six or seven people in each group.

Discuss the following questions in each group.

DISCUSSION

- What is one of your earliest childhood memories?

- What was your favorite game as a child? Why?

- Who were your childhood friends, and what are some of the things you used to do together? Are you still friends with them today? Why or why not?

- What is something you did as a child that got you in trouble?

- If you could be a child again what is something you'd do differently? Why?

- As a child, what did you think of God? How has your view of God changed through the years?

DECK OF SHARING

TIME: 30 minutes.

MATERIALS: a deck of playing cards and photocopy of "Card Questions" below for each group of four to seven.

VULNERABILITY: moderate.

DESCRIPTION

Form circles of four to seven people and give each group a deck of cards.

Tell kids to take all the face cards out of the deck and set them aside. Ask one person in each group to shuffle the cards and put them in the middle of the circle.

One by one, have each person choose a card and answer the question on the "Card Questions" handout that corresponds to the number of his or her card.

Go around the circle at least twice, giving everyone a chance to answer several different questions. If kids draw a number they've drawn before, they can return the card to the deck and draw another.

CARD QUESTIONS

- What is **1** achievement you're proud of?
- If you could change **2** things about school, what would you change?
- What are **3** ways to make you laugh?
- What is your routine be**4** you go to school in the morning?
- What were you doing in 198**5**? Be as specific as you can.
- What are your top **6** movies of all time?
- What is your favorite thing to buy at a convenience store like **7**-Eleven?
- How would you describe the perfect d**8** (date)?
- What's you favorite TV show on channel **9**? Why?
- Where do you see yourself **10** years from now? Explain.

EMOTIONAL GRAB BAG

TIME: 20 minutes.

MATERIALS: paper slips and a hat or box.

VULNERABILITY: moderate.

DESCRIPTION

Make a list of different feelings and write them on slips of paper, one feeling per slip. Here's a sample list. Add or subtract from it as you design your own.

- angry
- afraid
- extremely happy
- nervous
- bored
- bitter
- overwhelmed
- depressed
- at peace about everything
- embarrassed
- loved
- proud
- detached
- shocked

Put the paper slips in a hat or box so they can be chosen at random. Make sure you have enough paper slips for everyone in the group. It's okay to have duplicates.

Gather kids in a circle and let them each pick a slip. Give teenagers each a few moments to silently think of a time in their lives when they may have experienced that particular emotion.

Go around the circle, one person at a time, and have kids answer the first discussion question. Then, as a group, discuss the other questions. As always, encourage everyone to participate but allow people to pass if they desire.

DISCUSSION

- What's one time in your life when you experienced this particular feeling? How long did the feeling last?

- Was it easy or difficult to think of a time you experienced these emotions? Explain.

- Are each of these feelings appropriate to feel? Why or why not? What are healthy ways to express each of these feelings?

FAVORITES

TIME: 30 minutes.

MATERIALS: ball.

VULNERABILITY: low.

DESCRIPTION

Instead of asking the teenagers to form a circle, have them choose their favorite shape and ask them to sit in that configuration. For example, they might choose a diamond, square, rectangle, or octagon. The only requirement is that kids must sit facing one another so they can see one another's faces.

Give someone in the formation a ball. Ask that person a question from the discussion questions below, then have that person bounce or toss the ball to someone else. Have that person answer the next question. Continue until each person in the formation has answered at least one question. Give kids time to explain their answers, but keep the activity moving so there's little "dead air" time.

DISCUSSION

- What's your favorite TV show? Why?

- Who's your favorite teacher now? Why?

- Who was one of your favorite teachers in elementary school? Why?

- What's your favorite fast-food restaurant? Why?

- What's one of your favorite memories from last year? Why?

- What's your favorite movie of all time? Why?

- What's your favorite thing to do on the weekend? Why?

- What's your favorite breakfast cereal? Why?

- What's your favorite sport to play? Why?

- What's your favorite sport to watch? Why?

- What was your favorite toy as a kid? Why?

- Who's your favorite relative other than your parents? Why?

- What's your favorite subject in school? Why?

- Who's your favorite hero from history? Why?

- What's your favorite Bible story? Why? (Note: If your group doesn't know the Bible well, make sure you direct this question to someone in the group who can handle it.)

- Who's your favorite musical group? Why?

- What's your favorite song? Why?

- What's your favorite city? Why?

- What's your favorite vacation destination? Why?

FINISH THE SENTENCES

TIME:	30 minutes.
MATERIALS:	paper and pens or pencils.
VULNERABILITY:	moderate.

DESCRIPTION

Give each person a sheet of paper and a pen or pencil. Have kids complete the following sentences:

- Faith can help in tough times by...
- When I feel down, I usually...
- One thing that made me happy this week was...
- I think bad things happen to good people because...
- The best thing about morning is...
- I like weekends because...
- I dislike weekends because...
- My best friend reminds me of...
- If I could go anywhere in the next 30 days, I'd go to...
- I'd like to be like...

When kids are finished, form groups of no more than six and have kids each tell their group members how they finished five or six of the sentences.

Then have kids discuss the following questions in their small groups.

DISCUSSION

- How did you feel finishing these sentences? Why?

- What did you learn about yourself, others, and the group from this exercise?

- If you could write your own sentence starter that would help you understand others in the group better, what would it be? Why?

HEADLINES

TIME: 45 minutes.

MATERIALS: blank newsprint cut to the size of a newspaper, pens or pencils, old newspapers, and tape.

VULNERABILITY: moderate to high.

DESCRIPTION

Form groups of no more than five. Each group is a "news-gathering team." Give each team a couple of blank sheets of newsprint and several pens or pencils.

Say: **Each team is going to create a front page for a newspaper dedicated to the major events of the past year—not the events in the world but the events in your lives. To capture the headlines and the stories, you may interview your own team members or visit other teams to collect good stories.**

Have old newspapers available so kids can cut out words or titles to tape to their own newspapers' front pages.

Encourage kids to use one main headline and several smaller ones for the events that happened in the group members' lives over the past year. Ask teenagers to write brief descriptions of each event beneath the headlines.

Give teams about 35 minutes to work on news-gathering and headline- and story-writing. Then have teams join together to form one large circle.

Go around the circle and have team members present their front pages to the whole group.

Then discuss the following questions.

DISCUSSION

● What have you learned about the past year in the lives of the members of this group?

● What were high points of the past year? What were low points?

● What events do you look forward to seeing in next year's headlines?

● How did you see God acting in our group over the past year?

● How has your personal faith grown over the past year?

● What did you learn about the group from this activity?

HOW DO YOU FEEL WHEN . . .

TIME: 30 minutes.

MATERIALS: none.

VULNERABILITY: moderate.

DESCRIPTION

Form groups of no more than four. Have kids take turns answering the first question from the "How do you feel when . . ." questions in their small groups, then move on to the next question.

How do you feel when . . .

> your brother or sister gets more attention than you?
> your favorite team loses a close game?
> your teacher corrects you in public?
> your teacher praises you in public?
> your best friend dumps you for another?
> you succeed at a task for the first time?

When you've asked each of these questions, form new groups of no more than four to discuss the following questions.

DISCUSSION

- How important is it to reflect on your feelings? Explain.

- What did you learn about yourself from this exercise?

- What did you learn about others in our group?

- Describe one of the most intensely happy days in your life. Why was it such a good day?

- How can we learn from our feelings?

NEVER

TIME: 20 minutes.

MATERIALS: 10 M&M's candies per person.

VULNERABILITY: low to moderate.

DESCRIPTION

Form a circle. Give each person 10 M&M's candies.

Say: **We're going to go around the circle and say things we've never done. For example, you might say, "I've never visited Alaska" or "I've never fallen asleep in English class" or "I've never read the New Testament." Any person in the circle who _has_ done that thing must eat one piece of candy. We'll continue until only one person has any candy left.**

Remind kids to say things that won't embarrass others. For example, saying "I've never had sex" might be true, but could embarrass other kids.

DISCUSSION

● How did you feel during this activity? Were you worried you would have to admit something about yourself you didn't want to give away? Why or why not?

● What is something you've never done that you'd like to do?

● What surprised you most about this activity?

● What's more important in life: doing positive things or avoiding doing negative things?

LIFELINE

TIME: 30 minutes.

MATERIALS: tape, newsprint, and crayons.

VULNERABILITY: moderate to high.

DESCRIPTION

In this activity, kids will create "lifelines" by drawing continuous lines to represent significant moments in their lives. Lifelines can include straight lines, curved lines, spirals, sharp turns, circles, and anything else kids think of. Symbols, words, and different colors may be used to indicate specific events or feelings. The only requirement of a lifeline is that it must have a clear beginning (representing the person's birth) and a clear ending (representing the present day).

Tape sheets of newsprint around the room and have crayons available for kids to use. Give teenagers 10 to 15 minutes to draw their lifelines. Then form small groups of no more than five and have group members take turns describing their lifelines. Have teenagers answer the first three discussion questions in their small groups. Then form one large group to discuss the rest of the questions.

DISCUSSION

● What does this time line say about your life?

● Where along your time line do you see God working in your life? Explain.

● What direction do you see your lifeline taking in the future?

● How was this experience positive or negative?

● What did you learn about God? yourself? life? others?

MORE FORCED CHOICES

TIME:	30 minutes.
MATERIALS:	none.
VULNERABILITY:	moderate.

DESCRIPTION

Have everyone stand in the center of the room.

Say: **I'm going to read pairs of words. People who think the first word best describes them must stand on one side of the room, and people who think the second word best describes them must stand on the opposite side of the room. You may not remain neutral; you must choose one of the two words.**

After each "forced choice" have kids take turns telling the other people at their end of the room why that word best describes them. Or (if the group is fairly evenly split) have kids meet individually with members of the opposite side and explain their reasons to each other.

Begin each of the choices below with the question, "Which of the following choices best describes you?" Remind kids they aren't to choose the thing they *like* the best, but the thing that *describes* them best.

parakeet or eagle
sleeping bag or water bed
crocodile or frog
fall or spring
grandfather clock or sports watch
noon or midnight
rap or elevator music
football or badminton
tuba or violin
television or a book
Washington, D.C., or Hollywood
New York City or Small Town, U.S.A.
Diet Coke or Diet Pepsi
preparation or luck
plan ahead or spur of the moment
dog or cat
snapshot or videotape

business or pleasure
happy or sad
snowflake or hailstone
David or Goliath
Mickey Mouse or Donald Duck
river or lake
camping tent or palace
loud or soft
sweet or spicy
computer hardware or computer software
poodle or pit bull

After 10 or so forced choices, form groups of no more than six to discuss the following questions.

DISCUSSION

- Which choices were easiest for you? Which were most difficult?

- What did you discover about our group through this activity?

- How did you feel when you were in the smaller group? How is that like the way you feel when you stand up for something that only a few people in your peer group agree with?

- How is being a Christian like being in the smaller group? the larger group?

- How did you feel when you were in the larger group? How is that like the way you feel when you're in the majority among your peers?

ONE ON ONE

TIME: 35 minutes.

MATERIALS: Bibles.

VULNERABILITY: moderate to high. This activity could be scary for some people, and it's important to be sensitive to that. As the group becomes more of a community this activity can easily become a deeper sharing exercise.

DESCRIPTION

Have kids form pairs with people they don't know very well. Discourage them from teaming up with close friends.

Explain that this is an opportunity for everyone to get to know one other member of the group better. Say: **For the next 25 minutes** (or 10 to 15 minutes if you're using this with a junior high group) **you're to get to know your partner as well as you can. Find a comfortable space to sit and talk and learn all you can about each other.**

Encourage kids to share things such as where they grew up, what activities they enjoy, what their family makeup is, who their best friends are, and what they want to do in the future. Remind kids that this isn't a race to see who can learn the most in the shortest time. Help kids who might need additional prompting with things to talk about.

After 25 minutes, have the group form a circle to discuss the following questions. If your group is larger than eight, form smaller groups of no more than six to discuss the questions.

DISCUSSION

● How did you feel when you discovered what we were doing in this activity? How is that like or unlike the way you feel when you meet someone in everyday life?

● Is it difficult to get to know other people? Why or why not? What methods do you use to get to know others? What methods that others use make you most uncomfortable?

● What are the barriers that keep us from getting to know one another better?

● How difficult is it for someone who's new to get to know people in this group? How closed or open are we?

● Read Philemon 4-21 and discuss Paul's view of Christian relationships. How can this passage help you make friends with people who have few friends?

SHOW AND TELL

TIME: 30 minutes.

MATERIALS: none.

VULNERABILITY: low.

PREPARATION: A week before this exercise, send kids each a postcard asking them to bring one item from home that represents who they are. This item could be a childhood toy, a photograph, or anything else that accurately represents the person and his or her interests.

DESCRIPTION

Gather the group in a circle. Form multiple circles of no more than six if your group is larger than eight. One by one have group members present their items and tell their personal significance. Encourage others to ask questions.

Teenagers who forget to bring items can tell about something they would've brought if they'd remembered.

After the presentations, have kids discuss the following questions in their circle groups.

DISCUSSION

● What can you remember bringing for Show and Tell in elementary school? Why was the item significant then?

● Ten years from now, what might you bring to a Show and Tell time? 20 years from now? 50 years from now?

● What do the things we surround ourselves with say about our lives?

VARIATION

If you'd like to do this activity on successive weeks, you can be specific about the items kids are to bring. One week, have kids each bring a photo; another week, have them bring something from a hobby; and another week, have them bring something from their closets. Have fun with the categories you suggest, and kids will enjoy getting to know each other from a variety of perspectives.

WHAT HAPPENED?

TIME: 30 minutes.

MATERIALS: Bibles, note cards, marker, and tape.

VULNERABILITY: low.

DESCRIPTION

On note cards, list significant events that happen in teenagers' lives. Use the following list as a starting point. Add more of your own ideas, too.

- My girlfriend (or boyfriend) just broke up with me.
- I got straight A's on my report card.
- I flunked a class at school.
- My parents just got divorced.
- I've been accepted to a good college.
- I'm going to Disneyland.
- I just graduated from high school.
- I won the MVP award on a sports team.
- I was just cut from a sports team.
- I just got in a huge fight with my parents.
- I got a speeding ticket.
- My grandfather died.
- I'm having trouble with friends pressuring me to take drugs.

Gather the group members and tape one of these significant events on each person's back.

Say: **The object of this activity is to determine what's written on the card taped to your back. You may ask each person in the group one yes-or-no question to determine the event listed on your card, but don't be obvious in giving away other people's events. Mingle with the group and treat one another as if each person is really dealing with the event listed on his or her back. For example, if someone's card states, "My boyfriend** (or girlfriend) **just broke up with me," you'll want to comfort that person.**

When all the kids have correctly guessed their events, gather in circles of no more than seven and have kids tell if the events listed on their cards have actually happened to them. Then have kids take turns answering the following questions in their groups.

DISCUSSION

● What was difficult about this activity?

● How did you feel as you tried to guess your event? When in everyday life have you felt similar feelings?

● How did group members react to the event taped on your back? Is that the way you would want to be treated if the event had actually happened to you? Why or why not?

● Read Isaiah 63:7-9. How can we apply the way God treats us in tough times to the way we treat others?

WHAT WOULD YOU DO?

TIME: 45 minutes.

MATERIALS: Bibles.

VULNERABILITY: low.

DESCRIPTION

Form a circle.

Say: **I'm going to describe a variety of situations and then ask what you'd do in each one. After I've described a situation, I'll tap one person on the shoulder, and that person must say what he or she would do. That person will then tap someone else to hear that person's response. Don't just tap the person next to you, but vary who you choose. We'll continue until three or four people have responded to each situation.**

● Situation #1: **You're about to embark on a 3,000-mile journey across the country in a car. You can choose one tape to listen to on the car stereo. Which tape would you choose and why?**

● Situation #2: **You've been given one day to live. You have no financial limits on what you can do with that one day. Where would you go, and what would you do?**

● Situation #3: **You've just won $10 million in the lottery. What will you do with the money?**

● Situation #4: **You and your best friend are abducted by terrorists. They tell you that one of you must die. You both get to decide who it will be—you or your friend. How will you and your friend determine what to do?**

● Situation #5: **You can go back to any point in history and spend a day. What point in history would you go back to and why?**

Be sure each person in the group has a chance to respond to at least one situation. Then discuss the following questions as a group.

DISCUSSION

● What things do you consider when making an important decision?

● What's one tough choice you've had to make in the past? What made it difficult?

● Read Job 28:20-28. Why is wisdom in decision-making sometimes hard to find?

● Which of the situations we talked about earlier do you wish you were actually in? Why?

● Which of the situations forced the hardest choice? Explain.

● What is one decision you are wrestling with now? When do you need to make it? How are you going about it?

WHODUNIT?

TIME: 20 minutes.

MATERIALS: a slip of paper for every member of the group, pencils, and a hat or container.

VULNERABILITY: low to moderate.

DESCRIPTION

Give everyone a slip of paper and a pencil and have them each write an embarrassing moment they've experienced that no one else in the group knows about. Tell kids the moment can be a childhood experience or one that happened in more recent years. Ask kids not to identify names or places on their slips.

Collect the slips and put them in a hat or container so they may be chosen at random.

Read each slip aloud and have kids attempt to figure out whose embarrassing moment is listed. Give three teenagers a chance to guess each situation. If they're incorrect, have the "guilty" party reveal his or her identity. After all the slips have been read, form groups of no more than four to discuss the following questions.

DISCUSSION

- What, if anything, surprised you about this activity?

- How did you feel when your embarrassing moment was guessed? How is that like the way you felt when the event actually occurred?

- How can we help each other overcome embarrassing situations?

WISH LIST

TIME: 30 minutes.

MATERIALS: paper and pencils.

VULNERABILITY: moderate.

DESCRIPTION

Give each person a sheet of paper and a pencil.

Ask kids to write the following headings on their papers and leave space after each heading.

- family
- school
- friends
- God
- miscellaneous

Say: **Under each heading, write two wishes you'd like to make relating to that category. For example, under the school heading you might write, "I wish I would get an A in world history" or "I wish I didn't have to go to PE anymore." The miscellaneous category can be for any two wishes you want.**

After giving kids a few minutes to list their wishes, form groups of no more than six. Have kids each share three of their wishes from any of the categories. Tell kids they don't have to share if they feel uncomfortable doing so.

Then have kids discuss the following questions.

DISCUSSION

- What can you do to make some of your wishes come true?

- What might God think about your wish list? How could God help you with some of your wishes?

- What's good about making wishes? What's bad? How can you turn wishes into realistic goals?

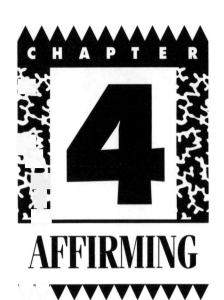

CHAPTER 4

AFFIRMING

Mark Twain once said, "I can live for two months on one good compliment." Bruce Larson, a pioneer in the small-group movement in the church, said, "It takes 10 'atta boys' to make up for one 'you jerk.' "

Many teenagers today get more "you jerks" than they do compliments.

Teenagers not only fail to receive compliments from others but also are reluctant to compliment themselves. Most teenagers are simply too tough on themselves and the people around them. They emphasize blame and de-emphasize praise. But when someone breaks through with an affirmation or encouragement, teenagers find themselves freed to be the people God intended them to be.

Paul recognized this need for affirmation when he penned these words: "So encourage each other and give each other strength, just as you are doing now" (1 Thessalonians 5:11).

Affirmations are important to the health of a group and the individuals within the group. The affirmation exercises in this chapter encourage group members to express their appreciation to one another. Affirmations also help teenagers become "people of affirmation"—people who know how to encourage each other just as Paul describes in 1 Thessalonians.

HOW TO USE THE AFFIRMING EXERCISES

1. Set the stage for affirmations. By being loving, affirming, and accepting even before the first step of bond building, you set the stage for the third step: affirming. Be careful in all of your youth ministry not to use putdowns. Not only do they hurt the objects of the putdowns, but they give implicit permission for your group members to use them, too. Don't even use putdowns for humorous reasons. Instead, be a person who affirms consistently and constantly.

2. Don't teach content during the affirmation time. Teach students to become affirmers but don't dwell on "teachable moments" in these activities. The goal is to affirm, compliment, and accept kids. There's plenty of time for teaching in other activities. Save the affirming activities for just that—affirming kids.

3. Encourage students to speak directly to

the people they're affirming. Help kids develop a "first-name vocabulary." An affirmation such as "Jeff, you really are a good listener" is infinitely more valuable than an affirmation such as "He listens well."

4. Encourage students to keep *all* their comments positive. Help kids learn how to focus on the positive without feeling like they have to qualify their compliments with negative statements. For example, saying "I really like you now, but I sure disliked you when you first came" can do as much harm as good. Putdowns cloaked in affirmations are still putdowns.

5. Encourage individuals to be specific. Instead of saying, "I like your attitude," encourage students to say something like "I like the way you're so conscious of people's needs and are willing to serve them. You encourage and inspire me by the way you do that." Give kids examples of specific affirmations in the way you affirm them.

6. Encourage students to accept the affirmations they are given. Remind participants of the rule in affirmation exercises: Compliments and affirmations cannot be denied; they're simply statements of how one person perceives another. A person's perceptions are not debatable. A simple "thank you" is the best response to an affirmation. Anything more or less is unnecessary.

7. Discourage students from affirming that which is an uncontrollable trait or characteristic. Affirmations should focus on inner characteristics or external actions. Giving positive feedback about an individual's physical appearance, for example, often causes a person's self-worth to revolve around his or her attractiveness. Instead, encourage affirmations that help kids feel good about their actions and attitudes.

8. Discourage individuals from using comparisons. "Stan, you're even better at doing skits than Jill" might make Stan feel good, but at Jill's expense. Even "You're the smartest person in the 10th grade" makes the person's success relative to those around him or her. It's better to say, "I appreciate your quick mind and the way you devote yourself to studies."

9. Participate yourself. It's important that you take every opportunity to affirm individuals and the group as a whole. Modeling appropriate affirmation behavior is one of the best ways to encourage kids to be affirmers, too.

10. If students have a difficult time *saying* affirmations, let kids *write* them. Younger kids often have a difficult time thinking of affirmations and an even more difficult time saying them. Give junior highers (and shy senior highers) time to write their affirmations.

11. Include God. Help teenagers learn to praise God by focusing on God as the recipient of their affirmations.

Keep these suggestions in mind as you move through step three—affirming.

APPLAUSE METER

TIME: 5 minutes.

MATERIALS: none.

DESCRIPTION

This affirmation can be done quickly and at any time in a meeting. Call the person (or persons) you'd like to affirm to the front of the group. Announce the reason for the affirmation. For example, you might say, "Mark and Terri did a great job decorating the youth group room. Let's give them a round of applause."

As the group applauds, pretend your arm is an indicator on an applause meter. Move your arm from right to left depending on the intensity of the clapping (see the illustration). Don't let kids stop cheering and clapping until the meter reaches its maximum.

VARIATION

Put a person in the "hot seat" in front of the group. Ask group members to describe the things they like about that person.

When group members finish, have them give the person being honored a round of applause. Use the applause meter with this, too.

AUTO AFFIRMATIONS

TIME: 25 minutes.

MATERIALS: photos of cars and specific car parts (brochures for new cars usually have great pictures and diagrams).

DESCRIPTION

Form groups of no more than seven.

Give each group a brochure of a new car or photos of cars and specific car parts.

Have kids take turns saying what parts of a car the others in the group are most like and why. For example, "Wendy, you're the head-lights because you always provide real insight when I need to make a decision." Or "Michael, you're the shock absorbers because you make a ride smoother when things are disrupted."

Remind kids to be positive in their affirmations and require each person to affirm everyone in the group.

BALLOON AFFIRMATIONS

TIME: 20 minutes.

MATERIALS: pencils, slips of paper, balloons, a hat, and a pin.

DESCRIPTION

Distribute pencils, two slips of paper, and two uninflated balloons to each person. Have kids each write their name on two slips of paper. Collect the paper slips and mix them up in a hat. Have kids each draw two names from the hat and write affirmations about those people on the other side of the paper slips. (If kids draw their own names, have them draw again.) Remind kids to say positive things. Have kids insert the affirmations into their balloons, blow up the balloons, and tie them off.

Have kids form a circle and bat the balloons around for several minutes. Then ask members to grab two balloons each. One by one, have kids pop the balloons with a pin and read aloud the affirmations and the names.

VARIATION

Tell kids not to read the names of the people being affirmed. Instead, have group members guess who's being affirmed. That way, affirmations are multiplied as more than one person is affirmed by the statements. When the guessing ends, ask the person holding the affirmation to read the name.

BIBLICAL AFFIRMATIONS

TIME: 10 minutes.

MATERIALS: 3×5 cards, Bibles, and pencils.

PREPARATION: With the help of your leadership team, choose a verse to affirm each member of your group. For example, you might choose Philippians 1:3, "I thank my God every time I remember you," for someone you've been especially thankful for in your group. You might choose Philemon 4-5, "I always thank my God when I mention you in my prayers, because I hear about the love you have for all God's holy people and the faith you have in the Lord Jesus," for someone who's been especially good at sharing faith with others. Match the verses to the individuals as much as possible. Write the scripture reference you've selected for each person on a 3×5 card along with his or her name.

DESCRIPTION

Form pairs and give each person a Bible and a pencil. Then give each teenager his or her partner's 3×5 card. Have teenagers look up and read aloud their partners' affirmation verses. Then have kids write their own verses on their cards to carry with them as encouraging reminders of their strengths, abilities, and value to God and the youth group.

BUTTERFLY

TIME: 15 minutes.

MATERIALS: none.

DESCRIPTION

Form a circle.

Say: **Some of us may feel like we're in the caterpillar stage of life. Or we may feel as if we're still wrapped up in a cocoon. But wherever we are in life today, someday we're going to have "butterfly" experiences. Let's think about what those experiences might be for each other.**

Say something you appreciate about the person on your left, followed by a description of a possible "butterfly" experience that person might have in the future. For example, you might say, "Heather, I appreciate your enthusiasm. Someday I believe you'll be an outstanding teacher and coach as you inspire others with your joy." Have kids continue around the circle, using the same "I appreciate ... Someday you will ... " format.

This affirmation may be more difficult for junior highers. You may need to help them by giving a few more examples of how to say the affirmations.

HAT OF COMPLIMENTS

TIME: 30 minutes.

MATERIALS: paper, pencils, 3×5 cards, and a hat.

DESCRIPTION

Assign each person a secret partner. Write the partner's name on a slip of paper and give each person his or her partner's name. Encourage kids to keep the names secret. Ask them to remain poker-faced throughout the name assignments.

Give kids a pencil and several 3×5 cards each and ask them to write positive characteristics of their partners by completing this sentence: "This person is..." Have kids write three or four positive characteristics about their partners (one per 3×5 card). On the back of the cards, have them write their partners' names.

Collect the cards and put them in a hat. You might want to read through the affirmations silently before you read them aloud to make sure the affirmations are appropriate.

Add a few affirmations of your own for group members.

Read each affirmation one by one and have teenagers guess who is being complimented.

Encourage people to call out guesses. This will not only affirm the person whose name is actually on the card but also those whose names are called out.

At the conclusion of the guessing for each affirmation, read the name on the card.

HUG YOURSELF

TIME: one minute.

MATERIALS: none.

DESCRIPTION

This quick affirmation can be done over and over again.

In the middle of a meeting or when the group has done well, yell out, "Let's everyone give ourselves a hug."

Have kids literally wrap their arms around themselves and squeeze. Even kids who feel uncomfortable about hugs won't mind hugging themselves.

LOVE LETTERS

TIME: 20 minutes.

MATERIALS: blank cards and envelopes, pencils, stamps, group members' addresses, and Bibles.

DESCRIPTION

Secretly assign each person in the group another group member's name. Don't let kids know who has their names. Sometimes it's a nice surprise for kids to receive affirmations from people they wouldn't expect to hear from.

Give each person a blank card and envelope, a pencil, a stamp, the assigned person's address, and a Bible.

Say: **Write a short letter to the person you've been assigned. Encourage this person by pointing out the qualities you like about him or her. Thank the person specifically for what he or she brings to the group. Then copy a Bible verse that will encourage him or her. I'll collect the cards and add my own note of appreciation before sending them.**

Have kids sign their letters, place them in the envelopes, stamp and address the envelopes, and give them to you sometime during the meeting. Ask kids not to seal the envelopes.

After the meeting add your own brief note of appreciation to each person's card. You may want to review the letters to make sure they're appropriate and uplifting. Several days after the meeting send the letters.

NICE NAME

TIME: 15 minutes.

MATERIALS: nametags and markers.

DESCRIPTION

Form groups of no more than four. Have group members brainstorm and choose positive nicknames for each other. The nicknames should reflect positive character traits or attitudes rather than physical traits or abilities that might be compared to others in the group. A nickname such as Soccer Stud might seem uplifting, but could secretly hurt another group member who yearns to be as talented in soccer. Remind kids to suggest only positive nicknames. For example, someone who has a warm smile and makes people feel comfortable might be called Smiley, Howdy, or Welcome.

Have kids make nametags using their new names and then introduce themselves to the entire group. Ask volunteers from each person's small group to explain why his or her nickname was chosen.

Explain that for the rest of the meeting kids must call one another by their new names. For fun, add a silly penalty for calling someone by his or her real name. For example, kids might have to stand on a chair and flap their arms like a bird or quack like a duck. Don't make the penalty too embarrassing, though, or you'll defeat the purpose of the affirmation.

STANDING O

TIME: one or two minutes.

MATERIALS: none.

DESCRIPTION

In the middle of meetings or events, call for a standing ovation for one or more members of your group. Explain the reason for the ovation and have kids all stand and applaud loudly.

Encourage individuals to call for standing ovations when they want to recognize a group member's accomplishments. Keep track of who's been appreciated so everyone gets a standing ovation at least once every few months.

TALK SHOW

TIME: five to 10 minutes.

MATERIALS: a tacky sports coat, desk, and microphone.

DESCRIPTION

For this activity, you'll need someone to act as a talk-show host. You can play the role, or you can let kids take turns as the host. Have the host wear a tacky sports coat during the interviews to add a bit of fun to the activity.

Choose two or three group members to be your "featured guests" each week until all group members have been featured on the "show." Don't let the featured guests know they're being featured until you announce "tonight's guests" at the beginning of each show.

Arrange your seating so the two or three guests sit next to the host, who sits at a desk like a television talk-show host. Have the other group members face the guests and act as the audience. Set up a microphone (it doesn't have to work) on the host's desk.

Have fun with the introduction of each guest. For example, play music as the guest enters and sits next to the host. To add meaning to the introductions, include a bit of history about each guest.

Have the host ask the guests questions about things such as their interests, dreams, favorite things to do, and families. Encourage the host to act as a real talk-show host might (without the putdowns). The host may also ask the audience to share some of the things they like and appreciate about the guest.

TOOL TIME

TIME: 30 minutes.

MATERIALS: a wide variety of tools, Polaroid instant-print camera, and film.

DESCRIPTION

Place the tools on a table in the center of the room.

Then have group members approach the table one at a time, select a tool, and present it to another group member with appropriate words of affirmation. For example, Scott might pick up a level and give it to Mark, saying, "Mark, you help me stay in balance, you help me stay on the level path with Christ, and I appreciate you." Or Carol might pick up a hammer and give it to Jackie, saying, "Jackie, you're so great at helping our group stay together when we start falling apart. You nail us together in the right places."

After each affirmation, take a Polaroid picture of the giver and the receiver with his or her tool. Then place the tool back on the table and have another person give a tool affirmation. To be sure each person is affirmed, tell kids ahead of time that it's their responsibility to make sure everyone gets at least one tool affirmation.

Have kids take their Polaroid photos home with them as reminders of the affirmations.

VARIATION

You can use this exercise more than once if you use different types of tools. For example, the group can use garden tools one time and construction tools the next. Consider tools used by doctors, athletes, and cooks, too.

TRADING CARDS

TIME: 45 minutes.

MATERIALS: a picture of each person in the group, scissors, heavy card stock, glue, pens, and baseball or football trading cards.

DESCRIPTION

During the week before the meeting send postcards reminding kids to bring wallet-sized photos of themselves to the meeting. If you think this might be too difficult, bring a Polaroid camera and take photos during the meeting.

Tell kids they're going to make a limited-edition collection of youth group trading cards. Kids may want to come up with their own brand name for the trading cards to add some fun to this activity.

Have kids each cut a piece of card stock to fit the size of their pictures and glue the pictures to them. Then have kids form groups of no more than five and sit in circles.

Say: **Work together in your groups to decide what information should be on the back of each trading card. Include "career" highlights, character strengths, and other positive things. Write the information on the back of the cards.**

Allow kids to refer to actual baseball or football trading cards so they can model their cards after them.

When groups finish working on their trading cards, gather everyone together and introduce each person by displaying his or her card and reading it. You may want to send cards home with kids or allow them to trade them with one another. Or you can display them in the narthex of the church for members of the congregation to read and enjoy.

VARIATION

Take a team photo and make a youth group team card. On the back of the card include highlights of group activities, best qualities of the group, and names of the "players" (if they'll all fit). Let the kids decide what they think is most important to include on the back of the team card.

Have kids make a card for the Manager or Head Coach (that's Jesus). On one side of the card have kids attach an artist's depiction of Jesus. On the other side, list important things about Jesus' life and teachings. Have group members decide which significant things to include in the card's limited space.

YEARBOOK AFFIRMATIONS

TIME: 20 minutes.

MATERIALS: a youth group yearbook (photographs and articles describing the past year's events photocopied and stapled together to resemble a high school yearbook).

PREPARATION: Plan this activity at the beginning of the school year. Assign a variety of kids to take black and white photographs of key youth group events and others to write short articles about the events. Have your photographers snap at least one photo of each group member (the sillier the better) before the end of the school year. Have a yearbook team put the articles and photographs together by cutting and pasting the photos and articles and photocopying them onto sturdy paper. Make enough yearbooks so each group member can have one.

DESCRIPTION

At a special meeting near the end of the school year, unveil the yearbooks and distribute them to youth group members.

Have group members sign one another's yearbooks. Let kids know they can only write positive things in one another's books. Kids will treasure these for years to come. This activity makes a great annual event and helps you build an archive of the ministry to youth at your church.

YOU'RE MY HERO

TIME: 30 minutes.

MATERIALS: paper and pencils.

DESCRIPTION

Form a circle and give each person a sheet of paper and a pencil.

Have kids each write the name of their hero (someone they admire greatly) and at least five things about that person they admire. A hero can be any person—living or deceased—who kids look up to and aspire to be like.

Go around the circle and have kids tell who their heroes are and what they admire about them.

After each person shares, have the rest of the group choose a characteristic that the youth group member has in common with his or her hero. Encourage kids to give specific instances when the person has shown his or her hero's admirable characteristic.

YOUTH GROUP WALK OF FAME

TIME: 45 minutes.

MATERIALS: for option #1: a large open area and wet cement or mud; for option #2: a "paintable" wall, paintbrushes, paint, and cleaning supplies.

DESCRIPTION

This activity is modeled after the Hollywood Walk of Fame. You can do this activity a couple of different ways. Both options are listed below.

Option #1: Prepare an area on your church property for a small square of concrete. Time the arrival of the kids to the time when the concrete is best suited for making hand prints (this will vary with the weather and the consistency of the concrete).

Have group members take turns making hand and footprints in the concrete and writing their names inside star shapes next to their prints. As each person adds his or her prints and name to the Walk of Fame, have the rest of the group say why that person's a "star" to them.

If you don't have the resources or space to use concrete, consider using mud for this event. Then you can play a game of mud football to "erase" the Walk of Fame.

Option #2: Get permission to create a mural in your church. A wall in the youth group room is often best for this activity. Provide paintbrushes, colorful paint, and cleaning supplies. Have teenagers take turns painting their names inside star shapes, then placing hand prints on the wall. As each person adds his or her print and name to the wall, have kids say why that person's a star to them.

ZOO KEEPERS

TIME: 25 minutes.

MATERIALS: none.

DESCRIPTION

Form groups of no more than five and have each group form a "cage" by sitting in a circle. Have the person whose birthday is closest to the last day of school stand up in the cage while the rest of the group sits around him or her. Then have kids take turns saying what kind of animal the caged person is most like and why. Remind kids to say only uplifting and affirming things. For example, someone might say, "Paul, I think you're most like an otter because you love to play" or "Leticia, you're a lion because you're strong and not afraid to stand up for what you believe."

Continue until each person has had a turn in the cage. For added fun, have kids first make the sound of the animal they think the caged person is most like.

CHAPTER 5

STRETCHING

When teenagers are placed in an unfamiliar and challenging situation they learn to explore alternatives, uncover and examine their fears, and come face to face with the possibility of failure. They also discover the trustworthiness of their peers—and of God. With the support of their peers, teenagers in unfamiliar situations often become "overcomers."

Stretching activities place group members in situations in which they must face and conquer obstacles outside their comfort zones.

Stretching experiences occur naturally among groups. Families experience stretching when finances fail, children are born, and relatives die. Amazingly, many families become closer during these times. And in the course of a long, hard season, athletic teams face challenges that often cause them to grow closer.

Unfortunately, most youth groups don't meet often enough for these stretching experiences to emerge naturally. It's imperative, then, for youth leaders to create fun and challenging exercises to stretch teenagers and help them grow closer to each other and to God. That's what this chapter is about.

A word of caution: Of all the steps, stretching requires the most energy and time to prepare and execute. But the effort is worth the trouble. Many of these experiences will be vividly etched in your kids' memories for years. And the lessons your kids will learn will help them grow and mature in their walk with Christ.

HOW TO USE THE STRETCHING EXERCISES

1. Carefully choose the experience. What proves to be stretching for one group may not be challenging enough for another. Use the knowledge you have of your group to make your choice of activities.

2. Work through the details well in advance. Most of these exercises can't be done with a half-hour's notice. Be prepared; get the help you need with plenty of lead time.

3. Be careful in your use of secrecy. Use discretion in deciding how much of an exercise will be kept secret from the participants and their parents. Some exercises work best as total surprises, but with others secrecy may cause problems. If in doubt, give advance warning to teenagers and their parents.

4. Adapt or alter the experiences. Some of the activities may be more feasible than others depending upon where you live and the resources available to you. Adapt the activities to fit your resources and environment.

5. Be aware of group size for maximum learning. The optimum group size for these events varies. Some can involve three or four people with great success. Others may require a larger group to be effective.

6. Schedule at least 30 minutes for discussion. These activities invariably produce teachable moments you can capitalize on to make important points. Schedule plenty of time for debriefing the experiences. Teenagers will want to talk about these experiences in great detail (especially if they've been building community through activities in the first three steps).

With these thoughts in mind, let's stretch!

ADOPT A FAMILY

TIME: two hours (preparation), two hours or ongoing (activity).

GROUP SIZE: four to 10.

DESCRIPTION

Students will come face to face with a family in need and be challenged to serve it. As a group, teenagers will decide how they'll serve the family and then carry out those decisions. Kids will grow and be stretched as they reach out to needy people in their own community.

PREPARATION

Make contact with a family or families in your community with specific, significant needs. You can get names from your church or a social-service agency in your city. Explain to the family that your youth group would like to help in specific ways, such as babysitting, fixing up the house, and doing yardwork. Be sure you have the family's support before announcing this activity to your group.

Tell the group about the family and its specific needs. Explain that it's up to the group to determine what to do to help. They might consider creating a work crew to do yardwork, forming a team for child care, or organizing a small group to clean the family's house. The only restriction is that the whole group must participate in some way and everyone must agree on what the group is going to do.

Encourage kids to be realistic with their ideas but avoid directing them too much. Letting *kids* decide what they'll do helps give them ownership of the effort.

After they decide on ways to help the family, help the teenagers create a specific plan for taking action on their ideas. Coordinate with adult sponsors to provide the supplies and transportation needed by the group. Let the teenagers communicate with the family to share their ideas and set up times and dates to help.

BEFORE THE ACTIVITY

● Meet with the group to go over the plan of action. Have kids discuss their feelings about helping the family in need.

● Spend time as a group praying for the family and its specific needs.

DURING THE ACTIVITY

● Allow students to follow through with their planning and preparation. This is *their* project.

● Arrange a time during the workday (or days) for the participants to stop working and get to know the family.

● Allow time for discussion and debriefing at the end of the project. Part of the discussion should involve a continued plan for reaching out to the family.

DISCUSSION

● How does it feel to help out a needy family?

● What surprised you about the family when you met its members?

● Do you feel like you made a difference in their lives? Why or why not?

● How would you feel if you were in need and a group like ours came to help?

● What was the most difficult aspect of planning this project?

● How did the group work together to prepare the experience?

● What are ways you can help people in need daily?

● What are specific needs you have that our youth group can help you with?

● How can we continue to serve this family?

● Read Matthew 25:31-45. How does this passage apply to what we did for this family?

ADVENTURERS

TIME: two to four hours (preparation), ongoing (activity).

GROUP SIZE: five or more.

DESCRIPTION

Teenagers will participate in a task force to plan and organize adventures and stretching activities. They'll grow as they reach out to the other members of the youth group.

PREPARATION

Tell kids you want to form a task force that will plan different adventures for the group.

Explain the commitment you'll expect from task force members. The following is an example:

● Task force members will meet weekly for six weeks. (Determine your own time commitment as well.)

● Meetings will include a Bible study on an adventurous life with Christ, a prayer time, and a planning time. The Bible study and prayer times will be led by different members of the task force. The planning time will be led by an adult sponsor and will focus on brainstorming ideas for group adventures.

● The goal of the group is to organize adventures for the group. An adventure is defined as any experience—such as hiking, skiing, canoeing, rock climbing, water-skiing, biking, going to a street mission, or visiting shut-ins—that challenges the group members. You'll have as much freedom as possible in designing your adventures.

Explain that the adventure task force will be fun but also demanding.

Challenge people to join the task force. If you have an overwhelming response, form more than one adventure task force.

Recruit an adult volunteer to lead the group (or groups) during the week.

Develop a Bible study series for the group to work through during their meetings. Let different kids on the task force take turns leading the Bible study and discussion time. Here's a sample Bible study outline:

The Adventures of Jesus Christ
Week #1—The adventure in the stables—Matthew 1:18–2:12.
　　　　Christ's Birth

Week #2—The adventure in the desert—Matthew 4:1-11.
Temptation
Week #3—The adventure on the Sea of Galilee—Matthew 14:22-36.
Jesus Walks on Water
Week #4—The adventures of the prodigal son—Luke 15:11-32.
Parable of the Prodigal Son
Week #5—The adventure on the cross—Matthew 27:32-56.
Jesus Crucified
Week #6—The adventure in heaven—Matthew 28.
Jesus Resurrected

BEFORE THE ACTIVITY

• Meet with task force members to plan a regular meeting time. Appoint Bible study and prayer leaders.

• Play games or do bond-building activities to help task force members get to know each other better.

• Pray together for the adventures that lie ahead.

DURING THE ACTIVITY

• Communicate frequently with task force members as they plan activities.

• Assist in the promotion of the activities.

• Plan a party after the task force's term of service is over. Use this time to celebrate the adventures that were planned and to evaluate the experience.

Use this activity four or five times a year so different group members can have the opportunity to lead the whole group in adventures.

DISCUSSION

• Why did you originally sign up for the adventure task force?

• What were three things you gained from being on this team?

• What did you learn about the adventure of following Jesus Christ?

• How can you keep your zest for adventure as you get older?

• What did you learn from this experience that you could apply in five years? 10? 20? 50?

• Would you recommend to other youth group members that they be on the task force ? Why or why not?

BIG BROTHER/ BIG SISTER

TIME: five hours (preparation), 1½ hours a week (activity).

GROUP SIZE: any number.

DESCRIPTION

Students will have an opportunity to share their time and talents with younger, less fortunate children. They'll develop significant relationships with kids who need attention and friendship. This stretching experience will give teenagers new insights into serving and living out commitments to others.

PREPARATION

Work within your church or through a social-service agency in your city to discover children who need big brothers or sisters. These might be kids from single-parent families or kids who simply need significant people to spend time with.

Contact the parents or guardians of these children and obtain permission to provide trained students to work with them.

At the same time, recruit and train youth group members to be part of the program. Big brothers and sisters must be mature (juniors or seniors are often best), and they must be willing to give 1½ hours a week consistently to one child for six to nine months. (Determine the length of the contract up front in consultation with the child's parents and the youth group member.)

Teenagers must also agree to attend three hours of training and a monthly meeting to talk about how things are going. Design a contract and have teenagers sign it.

Choose capable people—perhaps a child psychologist, a social worker, a children's pastor, or a parent—to help you interview and train potential big brothers and sisters.

Brainstorm activities big brothers and sisters can do with their little brothers and sisters in your area. Some ideas to spark your brainstorming: helping kids with homework, going out for pizza or hamburgers, watching appropriate videos together, playing basketball, completing art projects, visiting the zoo, and building snowmen or sand castles. Encourage your big brothers and sisters to come up with lots of new ideas.

BEFORE THE ACTIVITY

- Recruit big brothers and sisters and determine which little brothers and sisters to match them up with.
- Plan and implement your big brother and sister training program. Include general information about what is and isn't appropriate in this program. Help teenagers understand the children's needs. Consider having a social-service agent present to answer teenagers' questions.
- Pray for your teenagers.

DURING THE ACTIVITY

- Encourage teenagers to love their little brothers and sisters unconditionally. Ask teenagers to pray often for their little brothers and sisters.
- Meet monthly to discover how things are going in the program. Encourage the big brothers and sisters to talk about their experiences and learn from one another. Remind teenagers not to share confidential information about the children or their families.

DISCUSSION

- What were your expectations of this program before you got involved in it?

- How have those expectations changed?

- What's been the greatest joy about being in this program? What's been the biggest frustration?

- What have you learned about perseverance from this commitment?

- What have you learned that may help you if you ever become a parent?

- How has the rest of the youth group supported your efforts?

- How have you seen God at work in this experience?

- Read 1 Thessalonians 5:14-15. How does this passage apply to your work with your little brother or sister?

BIKE FOR YOUR LIFE

TIME: two to four hours (preparation), one or two days (activity).

GROUP SIZE: any number.

DESCRIPTION

Teenagers will bike a long distance together and learn to be a team. Kids may also raise money for a worthy cause.

PREPARATION

Plan a safe bike trip for your kids. Have biking experts in your church or community help determine an appropriate route. Have kids help you name the trip. For example, kids might call it RTP (for Redmond to Portland), Hot Wheels, or Bikers With a Purpose.

Determine whether the trip will take two days (recommended) or one day. Make your trip a challenge that will require people to train for at least a few weeks before attempting it. A 60-mile, one-day or a 120-mile, two-day trip may work for you depending on the terrain. Set a starting time and location and ending point (including a place to stay overnight if you're doing a two-day trip).

Arrange support services, meals, and refreshments for the trip. Consider a couple of motorcyclists to ride with bikers, a van with bike-repair tools, and a car with a bike rack in case a rider can't continue.

Prepare a comprehensive list of what each rider will need for the trip: a good bike (have them all checked by a biking expert), a water bottle, protein bars, proper biking attire, a helmet (required), a simple repair kit, and a spare tire tube. Check with a bicycle shop for more ideas on what you'll need.

Recruit a strong, experienced biker from your church to serve as the "expert" for the adventure.

If you want to make the bike trip a fund-raiser, have kids help you choose a project to support. Design a sheet for sponsors to sign pledging to pay a specific amount for every mile traveled. For instance, if the trip is 120 miles and a sponsor promises to pay 10 cents a mile, that sponsor would pay $12 upon the sponsored teenager's return.

Have someone in your group design a T-shirt for the trip. Provide T-shirts for all riders. You might establish a fee for riders to help defray the cost of the T-shirts.

Make sure the group is covered by insurance. Check with your church insurance agent for proper procedures.

BEFORE THE ACTIVITY

- Meet with group members three months before the trip. Explain the details of the trip and provide information kids can take home to parents. Encourage kids to begin training for the long trip.
- A month or so before the trip, meet again with the group to demonstrate how to do bike repairs. Use this time to see who's been training. If the ride is being used as a fund-raiser, encourage teenagers to begin getting pledges.
- About two weeks before the trip, finalize who will be going.
- Pray for safety and a great time. Pray for those people who will be helped by the proceeds from the pledges.
- Arrange transportation for the riders and their bikes if you're not returning by bike to the place from which you departed.

DURING THE ACTIVITY

- Begin each day with a devotion and prayer.
- Ride together. Don't let people ride too far ahead. If you have a few fast riders, let them go only as far as a mutually agreed upon checkpoint. Part of the lesson of the ride is that you're all in it together. So make sure that you're together or at least in groups of eight most of the time.
- Practice streamlining, which allows one rider to break the wind for the others by riding in front of them. Kids will need to take turns streamlining to give breaks to the leaders.
- Determine checkpoints where the van can be stationed with refreshments.
- Have someone take pictures of the trip.

Meet to debrief the event as soon as kids reach their final destination. Plan a celebration party a week or two later for kids and sponsors to view pictures and recall memories of the trip.

DISCUSSION

- Before the trip what apprehensions did you have? Why?

- How did you feel during the ride? Read Philippians 3:13-14. How does the message of this passage apply to your experience on the bike trip?

- What did you learn about God, yourself, and the group on this ride?

- How is life like a bike ride?

- What is one lesson you learned from this "ordeal" that you'd like to take with you in life?

CITY DIVE

TIME: two hours (preparation), at least 24 hours (activity).

GROUP SIZE: eight to 10.

DESCRIPTION

Teenagers will be challenged and changed as they experience the needs and problems of urban life. In a 24-hour period, through a combination of service, observation, and experience, teenagers will grow in their knowledge and understanding of the city.

PREPARATION

The City Dive places kids in the inner city for a 24-hour period (or more) to reach out in love to needy people. Find out if any organizations in your area have sponsored such a program before. Colleges and large urban churches often organize such events. If you find a program already in place, research it and consider plugging into it.

If you set up your own program, contact several social-service centers in an urban area near you and make plans for your group to take part in their service activities.

Here are a few activities to consider for your teenagers:
- plan and lead a church service at an inner-city mission,
- prepare and serve a meal at an inner-city mission,
- organize an outing or other activity with disadvantaged children,
- visit residents of low-income senior housing,
- walk the streets and observe the dynamics of street life.

Make arrangements for a place to stay overnight. One of the social-service centers or city churches might be interested. The closer you can get to what's happening on the streets, the better.

Brief the parents on the specifics of your plan. They'll want to know you've covered all aspects of safety, such as who will be leading the group, how each agency will work with the group, and the assurance of adult supervision.

BEFORE THE ACTIVITY

- Develop a schedule for the trip.
- A week before the outing, meet with teenagers who will be participating. Ask kids what they're expecting from the experience.

● Brief teenagers on what to bring. Limit each person to a couple of dollars, a sleeping bag, a journal, and a pen—the fewer supplies, the better the experience.

● Pray for the people of the city.

DURING THE ACTIVITY

● Begin with prayer.

● Follow the schedule and encourage kids to learn all they can about the needs of the city.

● Provide time for kids to write in their journals and discuss their experiences.

DISCUSSION

● Were you hesitant or excited to sign up for this activity? Explain.

● What were your fears as you entered the city?

● What was the most uncomfortable part of this experience? the least uncomfortable?

● How was the group a help to you?

● What are three things you learned from this experience?

● How has your view of the city changed?

● What was your most unforgettable moment in this experience?

● Read James 1:26-27. How is reaching out to people in need "pure religion"?

FEED OR WEED

TIME: two hours (preparation), eight to 10 hours (activity).

GROUP SIZE: any number.

DESCRIPTION

Teenagers will participate in a service project to the elderly in the community by working during the afternoon at the homes of elderly people and providing dinner and a program for them that evening. Teenagers will be stretched by reaching out to the elderly through physical labor and the preparation of a meal and program.

PREPARATION

Determine the extent of the service project, meal, and program your group will undertake. Many senior citizens can no longer take care of their homes and yards as they did when they were young. A weeding, mowing, and trimming party can make a big difference in these people's homes and lives. Consider washing windows, caulking windows, and painting trim if you have lots of group members.

Collect all supplies necessary for the workday, evening meal, and evening program and arrange transportation for kids and senior citizens.

BEFORE THE ACTIVITY

● Recruit teenagers to organize the work crews, food preparation, and evening program.

● Call the senior citizens to make sure they understand the project. Tell them when you'll arrive, how long you'll work, and that you'll be serving dinner to them that night. Tell them where the dinner will be held and determine their transportation needs.

● Have kids prepare a specific schedule for the day. Here's an example:

12:30	Meet at the church
1:00	Work teams begin the service projects; meal team begins preparation
5:30	Service projects end; workers clean up
6:00	Transportation of senior citizens
6:30	Dinner
7:00	Program begins

8:15   Program ends; transportation of senior citizens; workers clean up

9:00   Debriefing and discussion time

● Talk with teenagers about the needs of senior citizens and how this event will be an excellent way to acknowledge the wonderful service they've provided to others over the years.

● Plan the evening program. Encourage teenagers with musical talent to sing a song. Have others prepare skits. Remind kids to prepare a program that will cater to the interests of the senior citizens.

● Spend time as a group praying for the senior citizens.

DURING THE ACTIVITY

● Encourage teenagers to get to know the people they're serving.

● During the evening meal have students who aren't serving the meal sit with the people they served that day.

Return to the church after the senior citizens have been transported home. When cleanup is finished, debrief the experience with the kids.

DISCUSSION

● How did you feel as you served others today?

● What job did you like most today? least? Explain.

● What did you like most about serving the senior citizens?

● What surprised you most about this experience?

● What did you learn about growing old? What lesson can you take with you from this experience that will help you as you grow older?

TERRIFIC DAY CAMP

TIME: one to two days (preparation), three days (activity).

GROUP SIZE: one student for every three to five children in day camp.

DESCRIPTION

Teenagers will organize and lead a church day camp for first- through sixth-graders. They'll be stretched as they prepare an event they've never done before and as they work together to make the event a success.

PREPARATION

Contact a church in your area that's interested in having your group organize a day camp for them. You may want to use your own church, but working in unfamiliar surroundings with new people can enhance the learning experience and community building for teenagers.

Choose an existing curriculum for kids in first through sixth grade or have your kids develop their own using a variety of resources. Consider reviewing available vacation Bible school programs and books such as *Sunday School Specials* and *Quick Games for Children's Ministry* (Group Publishing).

Collect materials you think kids might need to prepare the day camp. Kids may require more materials as they develop their plan. Be prepared to help as needed.

BEFORE THE ACTIVITY

● Have teenagers meet a month before the camp to begin planning the event.

● Have kids help you prepare a schedule for the three-day camp. Review the sample schedule on page 112 for an idea of what one day might look like.

SAMPLE SCHEDULE

9:00 a.m.	Kids arrive and register
9:30 a.m.	Games and crowdbreakers
10:00 a.m.	Singing time
10:20 a.m.	Morning skit
10:30 a.m.	Bible lesson
10:45 a.m.	Craft time
11:30 a.m.	More games
12:00 p.m.	Lunch
1:00 p.m.	Outdoor activities (weather permitting)
3:00 p.m.	Day camp ends

● Appoint teenagers to roles such as teacher, crafts director, food preparer, songleader, and publicity director. Form teams to be responsible for each day's program elements.

● A couple of weeks before the event, schedule a meeting for teams to share their specific plans. Have kids collect necessary supplies by this time. Use this time as a "rehearsal" for the camp.

● Discuss with students their apprehensions about leading the camp.

● Spend time praying for all the day-camp participants—children as well as group members.

DURING THE ACTIVITY

● Allow teenagers to follow through on their planning and preparation. Offer help when needed but only to equip kids to lead. Don't take over.

● Allow 30 to 45 minutes for planning and prayer prior to each day of camp and for discussion and prayer at the end of each day.

DISCUSSION

- What was the most challenging part of leading the camp?

- How well did everyone work together in preparing this event? leading the event? How might the teamwork have been improved?

- Was it easy to work with the children? Why or why not?

- What attitudes and actions made it difficult to love the children?

- What attitudes made it difficult to love your teammates?

- Thinking of the children at camp, why do you think Jesus says in Matthew 18:3, "I tell you the truth, you must change and become like little children. Otherwise, you will never enter the kingdom of heaven"?

- What did you learn from the children?

UNDERCOVER

TIME: two hours (preparation), 1½ hours (activity).

GROUP SIZE: three to five per group.

DESCRIPTION

Participants will go undercover as they deliver food and gifts to needy families. They'll be stretched as they learn what it means to serve their neighbors without gaining recognition.

PREPARATION

Prepare a list of names and addresses of needy families or individuals in your area. If possible, obtain information about their specific needs.

BEFORE THE ACTIVITY

● Assign each group of three to five students the names of several families and information about their needs. Don't give more information than is needed by the students to do their job.

● Explain that each group will prepare and deliver care packages to the families on its list. Teenagers are to determine what's necessary in the care packages and how to obtain the items, (through donations or their own savings, for example).

● Assign drivers to deliver the groups to the neighborhoods where the needy families live. Supply maps if necessary.

● Encourage the students to begin praying for the families.

DURING THE ACTIVITY

● Have group members write an anonymous note to each family explaining the care package. Encourage kids to list a favorite scripture verse on the note. Have kids sign the note with their group name (something like The Undercover Kids or The We Care Kids).

● Meet at a designated time for debriefing after all the deliveries are made.

DISCUSSION

● How did you feel delivering the care packages without meeting the people? Read Matthew 18:1-4. How can humility help us as we reach out to others in need?

● What made it fun to deliver the packages?

● How do you think the people who receive these gifts will feel?

● What are other ways we can help people in need?

● Why is it important to reach out and help the people in our community?

● Read Matthew 6:1-4. Why does Jesus encourage us to do our giving in secret?

● Read the parable of the good Samaritan (Luke 10:25-37). Who are our neighbors?

● How does it make you feel to help your neighbor?

● What lesson did you learn from this activity that you can use for the rest of your life?

6

DEEPER SHARING AND GOAL SETTING

The time has come to move to the fifth and final step in the community-building process: deeper sharing and goal setting.

If your group has moved through the first four steps, the kids are probably less a "collection of individuals" than they used to be. Your teenagers have begun to develop a meaningful sense of community.

But for real community to occur, individuals must feel comfortable to share on a deep level. They must feel comfortable enough to risk sharing their deepest joys and most intense struggles. And they must become accountable to one another.

Most teenagers know the areas of their lives that need improvement. And they know they could use the help and support of friends to reach their goals.

That's the purpose of the activities in this chapter: to provide an environment in which honest, appropriate sharing takes place and teenagers bond together to care for one another.

The deeper sharing and goal-setting activities promote an atmosphere of encouragement and support. And the exercises encourage teenagers to verbalize their perceptions about current struggles and victories in their lives.

God bless you as you move to this step.

HOW TO USE THE DEEPER SHARING AND GOAL-SETTING EXERCISES

1. Work on goals that are measurable and realistic. "I will personally share my faith with every student in school" is a measurable and worthy goal, but probably not realistic. Help teenagers create measurable and realistic goals such as "I will share my faith with one of my friends this month."

2. Gently remind students which struggles are appropriate to discuss with the whole group. Problems that involve negative behavioral traits of *other* group members aren't appropriate to share with the whole group. Have kids avoid statements such as "I'm trying to be patient when Debbie gets possessive of our friendship."

Group discussions should also avoid intimate subjects a student may later regret discussing (such as sexual behavior). Do your best to keep the discussions from becoming an open arena for gripes about the school system, parents, or other popular complaints. Many of these subjects are best dealt with in a one-to-one setting.

3. Encourage teenagers to write down their goals. Goals are more easily recalled and evaluated when they're on paper. Once written, goals can also be placed on a mirror, in a car, or on a desk as a daily reminder.

4. Encourage teenagers to actively listen to one another. Deeper sharing means little to teenagers if they don't listen intently to one another. Remind kids of the concepts learned in the opening-up activities.

5. Model openness as a leader. Students will share only as deeply as you do. Talk about your goals. Ask kids to help hold you accountable to those goals.

6. Utilize teachable moments. In the final stage of community building, students are more open in their sharing. They feel comfortable enough with you and with one another to allow the group to probe and give some advice.

7. Give teenagers the freedom to fail. People don't meet *all* their goals *all* the time. Help kids pick themselves up after failure so they can move on to new—and successful—goals.

8. Adapt the activities and questions to your group. As always, you know your group best.

With these guidelines in mind, let's proceed.

AIRPORT

TIME: 45 minutes.

MATERIALS: a variety of sizes of paper and awards.

DESCRIPTION

Explain that you're going to have a paper-airplane-flying contest. Tell kids they can use any paper-airplane design they want and that awards will be given for the best airplanes. Have kids choose partners.

After pairs choose their paper, give them about 10 minutes to design and create their planes. Then call time and hold contests for things such as distance, acrobatics, length of time in the air, and design uniqueness. Also, give awards for the planes that flew the shortest distance, stayed in the air the shortest time, and were most dangerous to innocent bystanders. Make this a fun and upbeat time for kids.

After the awards, combine two or three design teams to form small groups. Have kids take turns answering and exploring the discussion questions.

DISCUSSION

● If your relationship with God were represented by an airplane, where would you be in flight? Which of the planes in our contest would your relationship be most like? Are you cruising at a comfortable altitude? Are you still on the runway waiting to take off or wondering if your plane can fly at all? Are you experiencing turbulence? Are you doing acrobatic tricks?

● If you were to get an award for the flight of your relationship with God, what would the award be titled?

● What can you see from your present location in flight? What are the big issues for you right now in your relationship with God?

● What are your flight plans? Where would you like to go in your relationship with God?

● What specific things can you do to reach those goals in your relationship with God?

● How can this group hold you accountable as you execute your new flight plan?

AND NOW THE NEWS

TIME: 1½ hours.

MATERIALS: desk, video camera, blank videotape, paper, pencils, sports coat, snacks, television, and video recorder.

DESCRIPTION

Arrange a "news desk" in a small room near your meeting place and set up a video camera facing the desk. Arrange the desk to look like what you see on the network news each evening.

Give each group member paper and a pencil. Tell kids they have 20 to 25 minutes to write short (no more than three minutes each) news reports formatted like those they might see on the evening news. Assign the categories of news, sports, weather, and editorials to different teenagers and give them the following instructions:

● In the news section kids must report on recent events in the lives of their families and friends.

● In the sports report kids must report on fun things they've done recently or are planning to do in the near future.

● In the weather report kids must describe their feelings in weather terms (sunny and bright, cloudy in the morning with sun by afternoon, and so on).

● Each person presenting an editorial must state and support an opinion he or she holds strongly.

Keep kids apprised of the time so they can be finished with their reports within 20 to 25 minutes. After they've completed their reports, have kids take a break for snacks or playing games. One by one, call kids into the next room to present their reports. Have a volunteer who knows videotape equipment record each news segment. For fun, have everyone giving a report wear a sports coat while delivering the news.

After kids have given their reports, gather the kids together in the meeting room around a television and watch the reports. Form groups of no more than six to explore the discussion questions.

If you have a large group, you might prefer to videotape the reports during one meeting and have the discussion during the next meeting.

DISCUSSION

- How did you feel as you recorded your news report? How did you feel as you watched the report with the whole group? How is that like the way you feel about sharing your deepest thoughts with others around you?

- On a scale of 1 to 10 (with 10 being very open and 1 being not open at all) how open would you say you were with your news report? Explain.

- Are you more open with your feelings and your life in a public setting like this or with one or two people? Explain.

- Is it necessary to broadcast to the whole world our deepest feelings and experiences? How do you determine who you share your feelings with?

- What did you learn about yourself from watching the video? Was that the real you on the TV screen? Why or why not?

- How much of your life do you share with God?

- How can this group help you become more (or less) open?

CONCLUSIONS

TIME: 10 minutes.

MATERIALS: none.

DESCRIPTION

This exercise should be used at the conclusion of a meeting, retreat, or stretching activity.

Ask group members to stand in a circle, join hands, and honestly finish the following statements.

Then close with prayer.

STATEMENTS

- Something I learned is...
- If I could tell my friends about this experience, I would say...
- Something I'll do differently because of this experience is...
- I could use your help by...
- You can count on me for...

DISASTER

TIME: 30 minutes.

MATERIALS: Bibles, markers, paper, and transparent tape.

DESCRIPTION

Form groups of no more than eight people each and have them sit in chairs arranged in circles.

Give each person a marker and sheet of paper. Ask kids to list the people, pets, and personal property that are important to them. Have kids scatter these names all over the paper. Give kids enough time to fill their papers with the names of the people and things they love the most.

Have kids fold their papers in half four times into small rectangles. Then have kids tear their folded rectangles in half. Tell them they can keep one half and must pass the other half to the person on their left. Have the people on the left place the passed papers under their chairs.

Say: **Because of events beyond our control, we've lost half of what we consider valuable. Open your papers and imagine what it would be like to have lost everything that was listed on the other half of your paper.**

Pause for a moment or two, then have kids take turns answering the first six discussion questions.

When kids finish discussing the first six questions, pass around transparent tape and have each person repair and return the torn page of the person on the right.

Then have group members answer the last two discussion questions.

DISCUSSION

- How is this exercise like real life?

- What or who did you lose in this disaster?

- When you realized your loss, how did you feel? If this had been a real-life disaster, what would you be feeling now?

- Have you ever been in a disaster in real life? What happened? How did it impact you?

• How do people cope with major losses such as the ones we simulated? Read Philippians 4:4-9. How can God help us deal with the disasters in our lives?

• How can *we* become more caring toward people in pain? What specific steps can we take toward reaching out in love?

After the papers are repaired discuss these questions:

• How have people "taped" your life back together in real life? How have you been the repair person in others' lives?

• How have you sensed God's healing touch in your life?

FRIENDSHIPS ON TARGET

TIME: 45 minutes.

MATERIALS: Bibles, paper, pencils, paper targets, and stickers.

DESCRIPTION

Give each person a sheet of paper and a pencil. Have teenagers create lists of the significant people in their lives. The lists can include family members, friends, and other important people. Tell kids they may each list no more than 10 people.

Give each person a paper target and 10 stickers—one sticker for each person on his or her list. Tell kids to write their own names in the center of their targets.

Say: **The center circle represents you. The surrounding circles indicate how close people are to you. Place a sticker on the target for each person on your list and write that person's name or initials on the sticker. The closer you feel to that per-**

son, the closer the sticker should be to the center of the target. The more distant you feel, the farther the sticker should be from the center.

When the targets are complete, form groups of no more than six and have them explore the discussion questions together.

DISCUSSION

- Looking at your target, who are you closest to? Who are you most distant from? What determines the difference in these relationships?

- What does it mean to be close to someone? Who are some of the people you've been close to in the past?

- If you could rearrange your target, who would you move and where would you move them? Explain. What can you do to make those changes happen?

- How similar to your placement of each person on your target do you think that person's placement of you would be on his or her target? Explain.

- Where would (or did) Jesus fit on your target? Read John 3:16. Where would God place each of us on a similar target?

- Why is it important to have close friends? How can this group help you become closer to the people you want to be better friends with? Be specific.

GOD AND ME: AN EVALUATION

TIME: 45 minutes.

MATERIALS: Bibles, "God and Me" handouts, and pencils.

DESCRIPTION

Give each person a "God and Me" handout and a pencil.

Give kids about 15 minutes to complete their handouts. Then form groups of no more than four. Have kids each share their answers to the handout questions. Then have kids take turns answering the discussion questions.

DISCUSSION

● What did you learn about yourself from this handout? What did you learn about your small group?

● What practical ideas will you commit to using to improve your relationship with God? How can this group support your commitment?

● Read Romans 8:38-39. How do the promises of these verses make you feel? What must we do to open our hearts to God's love?

GOD AND ME

1. What word picture best describes your relationship with God? (Some examples: a small boat in a heavy sea, running through a mountain meadow, climbing a tall mountain, riding a lion.)

2. What are the highlights of your relationship with God over the past year?

3. What were the most significant struggles in your relationship with God over the past year?

4. On a scale of 1 to 100 (with 100 being completely satisfied and 1 being absolutely dissatisfied), how satisfied are you with your relationship with God? Explain.

5. On a scale of 1 to 100 (with 100 being completely satisfied and 1 being absolutely dissatisfied), how satisfied do you think God is with your relationship? Explain.

6. What are three practical steps you can take to be more satisfied with your relationship with God?

HOW ARE WE DOIN' INVENTORY

TIME: 40 minutes.

MATERIALS: "How Are We Doin'?" handouts, pencils, a marker, and newsprint.

DESCRIPTION

Give each person a "How Are We Doin'?" handout and a pencil. Explain that the handout is designed to reveal the strengths and weaknesses of the group. Encourage kids to respond openly.

Collect the inventories and tally the results. If yours is a large group, get a few volunteers to help you while the group enjoys snacks or plays games. Or you can tally the results one week and report them the next.

When the results are tallied, present them to the group. Discuss the handout questions and highlight the scores that were highest and lowest. Use the discussion questions to help explore kids' feelings about the handout results. List the strengths and weaknesses of your group on a sheet of newsprint. *Praise the strengths and encourage the group in its weaknesses!* This is extremely important since groups can become hypercritical. Make sure there's a good balance between the positive and negative comments.

Have kids discuss the ways the group can maximize its strengths and improve its weaknesses. Write specific goals on newsprint and keep the goals posted in your meeting room as a constant reminder.

DISCUSSION

● What are our greatest strengths as a group? Explain.

● What are our greatest weaknesses? Explain.

● What specific goals can we set to maximize our strengths? to improve our weaknesses?

● Are we as open with new people as we are with existing group members? How do you think a newcomer to our group would respond to the survey?

● What issues weren't on the handout that we should address?

● What can each person here do to improve our group?

HOW ARE WE DOIN'?

Beside each statement write a number to indicate how true this statement is of our group. Your responses will be anonymous.

1—not true at all   3—somewhat true
2—seldom true   4—mostly true
            5—always true

Our youth group

_____ makes me feel welcome and comfortable.

_____ provides me with opportunities to learn about myself.

_____ provides me with opportunities to learn about God.

_____ is a loving community.

_____ involves everyone equally.

_____ is a place where I'm comfortable sharing my true feelings.

_____ is a place I'd like to invite my friends to share.

_____ considers my ideas and opinions valuable.

_____ is something I look forward to every week.

_____ has provided me with strong friendships.

_____ spends the right amount of time doing activities.

_____ spends the right amount of time in discussion.

KEEP YOUR BALANCE

TIME: 30 minutes.

MATERIALS: Bibles.

DESCRIPTION

Have everyone choose a partner. Ask partners to stand a couple of feet apart facing each other. Have partners place the palms of their hands together and lean toward each other. Explain that the goal of the game is to make the other person lose his or her balance. This can be done by pushing forward so the opponent falls back or by snatching palms back to cause the opponent to fall forward. A person has "fallen" when his or her feet move from their original position.

Have teenagers switch partners and play this game more than once. You might want to make this into an elimination contest to determine the group champion.

Afterward, gather in groups of no more than eight for the discussion time.

DISCUSSION

● How did you do in the game? What were your opponents' strategies? your strategy? How effective were these strategies? What caused you to lose your balance?

● How did you feel when you lost? How is that like the way you feel when you lose balance in everyday life?

● What causes you to lose balance in life? What are the results of losing balance in life?

● What happens when your spiritual life is out of balance? What part does spiritual warfare (as described in Ephesians 6:10-18) play in your loss of balance?

● What are specific steps you can take toward leading a more balanced life?

● How can our youth group help you gain balance in your life?

● What are ways you can help others keep their balance?

LAND OF ME

TIME: 30 minutes.

MATERIALS: photocopied maps of your city and pens.

DESCRIPTION

Distribute a photocopied map of your city and a pen to each person. The map should include enough detail to enable kids to mark the locations of their homes and other key points of interest in their lives. If your local phone book has a good map, get permission to photocopy the map for this activity.

Say: **I'm going to call out locations for you to mark on your maps. Think about where in the city each location should be marked based on how you feel about it. Find and mark the location of**

● **your castle—the place where you feel most at home and comfortable** (pause after each location is read to allow kids time to mark the locations on their maps),

● **the swamp—a place you consider muddy and difficult to maneuver,**

● **the stadium—a place where you go for entertainment,**

● **the secret hiding place—a place where you escape,**

● **the threat to your kingdom—a place representing any threat to you, and**

● **the cathedral—a place you go to focus on God.**

When the maps are all labeled, form groups of no more than five. Have kids show and explain their maps to their group members. Then have kids take turns answering the discussion questions.

DISCUSSION

● What are similarities and differences in the way people labeled their kingdoms?

● What did you learn about yourself from this exercise?

● What (if any) rearranging would you like to do in your kingdom? Explain.

● Where do you spend most of your time on weekdays? on weekends? What can you learn about people from the places they spend most of their time?

● What might God want you to change (if anything) about your kingdom?

● What is one thing you've learned from this activity that you'd like to apply to the rest of your life? How can our group help you apply that lesson?

ISK

| **TIME:** | 30 minutes. |
| **MATERIALS:** | Bibles, "Risking Much" handouts. |

DESCRIPTION

Give each person a photocopy of the "Risking Much" handout on page 134. Ask them to follow along silently as you read it aloud.

Form groups of no more than four and have kids explore the discussion questions.

DISCUSSION

- Which risk described on the handout do you have the most trouble taking? Explain.

- Which risk is the most comfortable for you? Explain.

- What factors make it difficult for you to take risks? Why?

- Do you think it's important to take risks in life? Why or why not? What are appropriate risks? inappropriate risks?

- Read John 14:6. What is the greater risk: to choose to follow God or to reject God? Explain. What risks do we take when we live out our faith?

- What is one risk you've taken in the past? What was the result?

- What is one risk you need to take but have been avoiding?

- How can this group help you in taking that risk?

RISKING MUCH

To laugh is to risk appearing foolish.

To weep is to risk appearing sentimental.

To reach out for another is to risk involvement.

To expose feelings is to risk exposing our true selves.

To place our ideas and dreams before the crowd is to risk loss.

To love is to risk not being loved in return.

To live is to risk dying.

To hope is to risk despair.

To try at all is to risk failure.

But risk we must, because the greatest hazard in life is to risk nothing. The man, the woman who risks nothing does nothing, has nothing, is nothing.

—Author Unknown

SHIPWRECK

TIME: one hour.

MATERIALS: nametags, markers, and ice cream sundaes.

DESCRIPTION

Say: **You're aboard a ship that just struck an iceberg. The ship has been damaged beyond repair and is sinking. You're the only people left on the ship, and there is but one lifeboat left. Unfortunately the lifeboat can take only two-thirds of the people in this room. If the lifeboat takes any more, it will surely sink, and everyone will die in the icy waters.**

Help is on the way, but people left on the sinking ship will surely die. I'm going to assign each person an identity. During this activity, you must play the part of the person whose identity you've been assigned. Your job is to determine, as a group, who will go on the lifeboat and who won't.

Assign each person an identity from the "Characters" box. It's okay if more than one person has the same identity or if you use only some of the identities. Distribute nametags and markers and have each person write his or her identity on a nametag.

Tell teenagers that those on the lifeboat will get ice cream sundaes and those who are left on the ship will not. This will add incentive to want to get on the lifeboat.

Say: **You have 15 minutes before the ship is completely under water. I'll keep you posted about the remaining time, but when time's up, you must tell me which people will get on the lifeboat. If you can't agree at that time, you'll all go down with the ship.**

Occasionally remind kids of the time left. When time is up, ask kids to tell you who will be saved. Give those people ice cream sundaes. After the discussion, give the other group members sundaes, too. If your group members couldn't agree who would be saved, don't give any sundaes until after the discussion.

CHARACTERS

the ship's captain	high school student
doctor	journalist
1-year-old child	newly wed husband
1-year-old child's mother	newly wed wife
ship's mechanic	important politician
stowaway	retired businessman
millionaire	minister
accountant	father of two
teenager	school teacher
college professor	professional baseball player
mother of four children not on ship	lawyer

DISCUSSION

- How did you feel during this simulation? When in everyday life have you felt similar feelings?

- What helped you determine who would be saved from the sinking ship?

- How did you feel toward the people who ended up on the lifeboat? who didn't end up on the lifeboat?

- What made this a difficult exercise? What is one of the most difficult decisions you've had to make? How did you make that decision? Who helped you make the decision?

- What does it mean to sacrifice? When have you had to make some difficult sacrifices?

- Read 1 John 3:16. How does Jesus' sacrifice relate to today's activity?

- How is life like this experience?

WRITE ON!

TIME: one hour.

MATERIALS: blank journals or notebooks and pens.

DESCRIPTION

Give each group member a blank journal or notebook and a pen. If you wish, you can have kids make their own journals out of paper and card stock (for the covers). Have kids decorate their journals or notebooks to reflect their interests or hobbies. For example, someone who's interested in music might decorate his or her book to look like a piano.

Ask group members to write in their journals every day for a week (or longer). Have kids write the following categories on the first page of their journals to remind them what to write about: activities; relationships with God, family, and friends; feelings; scripture passages; dreams; concerns; and answered prayers.

The following week, form groups of no more than four and have kids share insights from their journals with their small groups. Then have those small groups dive into the discussion questions about the journal-keeping experience.

You may want to continue this activity for an entire school year and compile positive insights in a booklet to encourage kids through the summer or as they graduate.

DISCUSSION

● What did you enjoy about journal-keeping? What was easiest for you about the experience? hardest? Explain.

● What did you learn about yourself from writing in your journal?

● What faith insights did you gain from spending time reflecting on your relationship with God?

● What new goals and dreams do you have after this experience? How can the group help you reach those goals?

Tackle important issues in the lives of your teenagers with **Active Bible Curriculum**®. Help your teenagers learn the Bible and discover how to apply it to their daily lives. And save your church money—each book includes a complete teachers guide, handout masters you can photocopy, publicity helps, and bonus ideas—all for one low price.

FOR JUNIOR HIGH/MIDDLE SCHOOL:

Accepting Others: Beyond Barriers & Stereotypes, ISBN 1-55945-126-2

Advice to Young Christians: Exploring Paul's Letters, ISBN 1-55945-146-7

Applying the Bible to Life, ISBN 1-55945-116-5

Becoming Responsible, ISBN 1-55945-109-2

Bible Heroes: Joseph, Esther, Mary & Peter ISBN 1-55945-137-8

Boosting Self-Esteem, ISBN 1-55945-100-9

Building Better Friendships, ISBN 1-55945-138-6

Can Christians Have Fun?, ISBN 1-55945-134-3

Christmas: A Fresh Look, ISBN 1-55945-124-6

Dealing With Disappointment, ISBN 1-55945-139-4

Doing Your Best, ISBN 1-55945-142-4

Evil and the Occult, ISBN 1-55945-102-5

Guys & Girls: Understanding Each Other, ISBN 1-55945-110-6

Handling Conflict, ISBN 1-55945-125-4

Is God Unfair?, ISBN 1-55945-108-4

Peer Pressure, ISBN 1-55945-103-3

Prayer, ISBN 1-55945-104-1

Telling Your Friends About Christ, ISBN 1-55945-114-9

The Ten Commandments, ISBN 1-55945-127-0

Today's Media: Choosing Wisely, ISBN 1-55945-144-0

Today's Music: Good or Bad?, ISBN 1-55945-101-7

What Is God's Purpose for Me?, ISBN 1-55945-132-7

What's a Christian?, ISBN 1-55945-105-X

...and many more!

FOR SENIOR HIGH:

1 & 2 Corinthians: Christian Discipleship, ISBN 1-55945-230-7

Angels, Demons, Miracles & Prayer, ISBN 1-55945-235-8

Changing the World, ISBN 1-55945-236-6

Christians in a Non-Christian World, ISBN 1-55945-224-2

Counterfeit Religions, ISBN 1-55945-207-2

Dating Decisions, ISBN 1-55945-215-3

Dealing With Life's Pressures, ISBN 1-55945-232-3

Deciphering Jesus' Parables, ISBN 1-55945-237-4

Exploring Ethical Issues, ISBN 1-55945-225-0

Faith for Tough Times, ISBN 1-55945-216-1

Getting Along With Parents, ISBN 1-55945-202-1

The Gospel of John: Jesus' Teachings, ISBN 1-55945-208-0

Hazardous to Your Health: AIDS, Steroids & Eating Disorders, ISBN 1-55945-200-5

Is Marriage in Your Future?, ISBN 1-55945-203-X

Knowing God's Will, ISBN 1-55945-205-6

Making Good Decisions, ISBN 1-55945-209-9

Movies, Music, TV & Me, ISBN 1-55945-213-7

Real People, Real Faith, ISBN 1-55945-238-2

Revelation, ISBN 1-55945-229-3

School Struggles, ISBN 1-55945-201-3

Sex: A Christian Perspective, ISBN 1-55945-206-4

Who Is God?, ISBN 1-55945-218-8

Who Is Jesus?, ISBN 1-55945-219-6

Who Is the Holy Spirit?, ISBN 1-55945-217-X

Your Life as a Disciple, ISBN 1-55945-204-8

...and many more!

Order today from your local Christian bookstore, or write: Group Publishing, Box 485, Loveland, CO 80539.

PUT FAITH INTO ACTION...

...with Group's **Projects With a Purpose™ for Youth Ministry.**

Want to try something different with your 7th-12th grade classes? Group's **Projects With a Purpose™ for Youth Ministry** offers four-week courses that really get kids into their faith. Each **Project With a Purpose** course gives you tools to facilitate a project that will provide a direct, purposeful learning experience. Teenagers will discover something significant about their faith while learning the importance of working together, sharing one another's troubles, and supporting one another in love...plus they'll have lots of fun! For Sunday school classes, midweek meetings, home Bible studies, youth groups, retreats, or any time you want to help teenagers discover more about their faith.

Acting Out Jesus' Parables
Strengthen your teenagers' faith as they are challenged to understand the parables' descriptions of the Christian life. Explore such key issues as the value of humility and the importance of hope.   ISBN 1-55945-147-5

Celebrating Christ With Youth-Led Worship
Kids love to celebrate. For Christians, Jesus is the ultimate reason to celebrate. And as kids celebrate Jesus, they'll grow closer to him—an excitement that will be shared with the whole congregation.   ISBN 1-55945-410-5

Checking Your Church's Pulse
Your teenagers will find new meaning for their faith with this course. Interviews with congregational members will help your teenagers, and your church, grow closer together.   ISBN 1-55945-408-3

Serving Your Neighbors
Strengthen the "service heart" in your teenagers. They'll appreciate the importance of serving others as they follow Jesus' example.   ISBN 1-55945-406-7

Sharing Your Faith Without Fear
Teenagers don't have to be great orators to share with others what God's love means to them. Teach them to express their faith through everyday actions without fear of rejection.   ISBN 1-55945-409-1

Teaching Teenagers to Pray
Watch as your teenagers develop strong, effective prayer lives as you introduce them to the basics of prayer. They'll learn how to pray with and for others.   ISBN 1-55945-407-5

Teenagers Teaching Children
Teach your teenagers how to share the Gospel with children. Through this course, your teenagers will learn more about their faith by teaching others and develop teaching skills to last a lifetime.   ISBN 1-55945-405-9

Videotaping Your Church Members' Faith Stories
Teenagers will enjoy learning about their congregation members with this exciting video project. And, they'll learn the depth and power of God's faithfulness to his people.   ISBN 1-55945-239-0

Order today from your local Christian bookstore, or write: Group Publishing, Box 485, Loveland, CO 80539.

MORE INNOVATIVE RESOURCES FOR YOUR YOUTH MINISTRY

The Youth Worker's Encyclopedia of Bible-Teaching Ideas: Old Testament/ New Testament

Explore the most comprehensive idea-books available for youth workers! Discover more than 350 creative ideas in each of these 400-page encyclopedias—there's at least one idea for each and every book of the Bible. Find ideas for...retreats and overnighters, learning games, adventures, special projects, parties, prayers, music, devotions, skits, and much more!

Plus, you can use these ideas for groups of all sizes in any setting. Large or small. Sunday or mid-week meeting. Bible study. Sunday school class or retreat. Discover exciting new ways to teach each book of the Bible to your youth group.

Old Testament   ISBN 1-55945-184-X
New Testament   ISBN 1-55945-183-1

Clip-Art Cartoons for Churches

Here are over 180 funny, photocopiable illustrations to help you jazz up your calendars, newsletters, posters, fliers, transparencies, postcards, business cards, announcements—all your printed materials! These fun, fresh illustrations cover a variety of church and Christian themes, including church life, Sunday school, youth groups, school life, sermons, church events, volunteers, and more! And there's a variety of artistic styles to choose from so each piece you create will be unique and original.

Each illustration is provided in three different sizes so it's easy to use. You won't find random images here...each image is a complete cartoon. And these cartoons are fun! In fact, they're so entertaining that you may just find yourself reading the book and not photocopying them at all.

Order your copy of **Clip-Art Cartoons for Churches** today...and add some spice to your next printed piece.

ISBN 1-55945-791-0

Bore No More! (For Every Pastor, Speaker, Teacher)

This book is a must for every pastor, youth leader, teacher, and speaker. These 70 audience-grabbing activities pull listeners into your lesson or sermon—and drive your message home!

Discover clever object lessons, creative skits, and readings. Music and celebration ideas. Affirmation activities. All the innovative techniques 85 percent of adult church-goers say they wish their pastors would try! (recent Group Publishing poll)

Involve your congregation in the learning process! These complete 5- to 15-minute activities highlight common New Testament Lectionary passages, so you'll use this book week after week.

ISBN 1-55945-266-8

Order today from your local Christian bookstore, or write:
Group Publishing, Box 485, Loveland, CO 80539.